Keep Soaring!

Donna McSally

Mark Of An Eagle
How Your Life Changes the World

David McNally

Praise for *Even Eagles Need a Push*

"This is a self-help book that helps. Four stars!"

Larry King

"This book is full of questions, like a long conversation with a nosy but caring friend, or a psychotherapist (the therapist is the one you have to pay)...Better buy yourself a pencil to go with Even Eagles—a big eraser, just in case."

The Detroit News/Free Press

"Tremendous motivational material! I enjoyed it so much I've shared...it with my sales force."

Mary Kay Ash, Chairman Emeritus, Mary Kay Cosmetics

"Even Eagles Need A Push caused me to evaluate my life as well as my profession. It forces you to expand your horizons."

Lou Holtz, former head football coach of the University of Notre Dame and member of the College Football Hall of Fame

"This inspiring book speaks uniquely to today's educators. The ideas for achieving success and personal excellence are powerful."

Dr. Carol Roberts, Associate Professor, University of La Verne

Praise for *The Eagle's Secret*

"Each of us wants to thrive in our career and, more importantly, our personal life. David McNally provides a framework to define what that truly means and a wonderful road map to get there."

Roger Dow, Vice-President, Marriott

"The Eagle's Secret has had a huge impact on my career in professional sports. This is a mandatory read for anyone who wants to soar with the eagles."

Pat Williams, EVP, Orlando Magic

"David McNally's inspirational, proactive approach to business and life strategies permeates each chapter of The Eagle's Secret. McNally is a master communicator."

Rick Tippett, Director of National Advertising,
The Washington Post

"I keep The Eagle's Secret on my desk because I refer to it so often. David McNally has done a superb job weaving stories, exercises, and quotes into an inspiring text."

Ron Campbell, President, Center for Leadership Studies

"If you consider learning to be a lifelong process, then you will be flooded with new insights as David McNally takes you on a masterfully engineered journey of self-discovery."

Tim Foley, Crown Ambassador Distributors, Amway Corporation

Praise for *Be Your Own Brand*

"A strong personal brand is paramount for effective leadership. Be Your Own Brand is a powerful and practical guide for building deep and meaningful relationships."

Perry Cantarutti, SVP, Europe,
Middle East and Africa, Delta Air Lines

"Be Your Own Brand, when applied within a business organization, has the power to accelerate the pace of organizational brand development tremendously."

Taras K. Rebet, President, Western Europe,
Otto Bock HealthCare GmbH

"The one sales effectiveness book every sales and marketing executive should have on the bookshelf, Be Your Own Brand speaks to today's urgent business issue: your people are your brand. I found every page to be full of great ideas and powerful insights."

E. Patrick Gallagher, Director, Learning and Development.
FindLaw, a Thomson Reuters Company

Mark Of An Eagle
How Your Life Changes the World

David McNally

Wisdom
Editions

Minneapolis

Minneapolis

FIRST EDITION MARCH 2017

MARK OF AN EAGLE: How Your Life Changes the World

Copyright © 2017 by David McNally.

Printed in the United States of America.

10 9 8 7 6 5 4 3 2 1

ISBN: 978-1-939548-XX-X

Cover and interior design: David Bradley

To my grandchildren

Ellie, Evan, Liam, Sydney, and Fynn.

Acknowledgements

When I wrote my first book—*Even Eagles Need a Push*—I learned the power of critique. My willingness to submit the first manuscript to the eyes and thoughts of others enabled a book to be created that has sold hundreds of thousands of copies. I also discovered that people are kind, sensitive, and what was most helpful—ruthlessly honest.

This is the process I have now followed for all my books. These days, when there is so much to occupy our time, many people, once again, demonstrated the generosity to read this manuscript, provide feedback, and contribute to ensuring what you are about to read has integrity and addresses the subject matter with relevance and practicality.

By naming them, I honor their collaboration in this work.

Terry Ainsworth, Lisa Arie, Grayce Belvedere Young, Michael Boland, Janet Bunday, Drew Clark, Audie Dunham, Susan Fronk, Diane Goulding, Bill Gjetson, Sue Hall, Brett Haupt, Clive Hoffman, Elaine Kramer, Don McGrath, Kerry Olsen, Annemarie Osborne, Julie Paleen, Sarah Patnode, Carlos Sabbagh, Jim Secord, Julie Showers, Donna Shetler, Denny Smith, Jeff Smith, Wendy Smith, Hazel Stewart, Joy Szarke, Steve Wardleworth, and Cath Williams.

Throughout the book, you will read stories written by others about people who have left a special mark on their lives. I am deeply grateful to Rebecca Bond, Audie Dunham, Corky Hall, Mike Haglin, Cheryl Hauser, Sally Johnson, Bill Lentsch, Kerry Olsen, Jeannie Seeley Smith, Allen Shoup, and Peter Wilander for their contributions.

Persistence is a key ingredient for writing a book. Authors often need nudging—some might use the word pushing— to sustain that persistence. Rarely do any of us fail to experience moments of doubt, and so to be affirmed that one has something worthwhile to say is a vital impetus for not giving up and completing the product. My nudgers were my colleagues at TransForm Corporation, Sarah McNally and Pam Rusten, as well as the many friends and clients who encouraged my efforts.

Ian Graham Leask, my editor at Calumet Editions, brought a rigor and discipline to the words on each page. He offered alternatives that reduced my tendency to use certain words repetitively and, therefore, added an important variety to how I could articulate the points I was endeavoring to make.

The creative talents of Dave Bradley and Gary Lindberg provided the external and internal design of the book. One of the best pieces of advice I ever got from an established, successful author, was to make one's book inviting. Dave and Gary, I believe, have succeeded admirably in this regard.

You will see many other writers and thought-leaders quoted in the pages ahead. They deserve special recognition, for their words have influenced and inspired me as I hope they will you. I am clear that although this book is my own creation, it is built on the ideas and thoughts of people since humans first began pursuing an answer to the question: why am I here?

Let me add one final acknowledgment—perhaps even a toast: to the creative spirit that exists within each of us.

Contents

Preface

Everyone who has ever lived has left their mark on the world. Some marks may seem barely decipherable, and others have clearly changed the course of humankind. No matter one's level of drive or ambition, however, most of us want to feel that our lives matter, that our being here means something, and that there is a purpose for our existence.

In my previous books, *Even Eagles Need a Push* and *The Eagle's Secret*, I began with a story of one of my children. Now I have grandchildren. Much has happened over the intervening years.

Like most human beings, the highs of my life have been exhilarating and the lows exhausting, but I have learned not to label circumstances as good or bad. Both joy and pain are an integral part of this somewhat unpredictable journey, and I now know that accepting rather than resisting this reality is a key ingredient of a well-lived life.

Despite the wonders that surround us, there are those fond of saying there is nothing new in the universe. That staggers me. Aspiring writers are often discouraged by people suggesting that a certain subject or theme has been covered before so why bother? Your life and my life have never been lived before. That's what's new. What we create is truly original, and no one else can lay claim to that creation.

The most important question we can ask ourselves is therefore: what do I want to create? The desire and need to create is in our DNA. The decisions we make, the attitudes we hold, the behaviors we exhibit, create the depth of our experiences, the quality of our relationships, and the success we achieve. Who and what we are today is our own creation.

As a boy growing up in Australia, to envision the life I have now lived would clearly have been a fantasy. An entrepreneur, author of several books, documentary film producer, professional speaker—all of these were unimaginable. So was going broke, being separated from my family, losing my wife to cancer, and personally experiencing cancer.

I am deeply grateful to those who have left their own indelible mark on my life; they opened my mind and inspired me to push on and not give up. In turn, I write this book to open you to the possibilities for your life and to encourage you to push on no matter your current circumstances or the problems with which you struggle.

There is an urgent need for those who are willing to take on that challenge, who are unwilling to settle for mere existence, and who understand that human progress is propelled by those who, by their actions and example, create a better world for all.

Throughout the pages ahead you will be introduced to people who generously share stories of how their lives today continue to be positively influenced by a special person, one who left a unique mark. These marks have an undeniable ripple effect, and we are all the beneficiaries.

Leaving your mark, however, is not a goal to be set; it is a result. It is the outcome of realizing the enormous potential that exists within you, the belief that there is a special purpose for your existence, the awareness that you share responsibility for what happens in our world, and the commitment to fully utilize your gifts and talents to create a rich and rewarding life.

Prepare for the unexpected. We are embarking on an adventure that might take you into uncharted territory. You will be exploring questions that relate to how you desire to shape your personal and professional life. The responsibility for discovering what is important and meaningful to you is yours alone. Your heart, mind, and soul know how you want your life to look and feel.

Consider this book as a guide, one that allows you the freedom to take detours whenever an aspect of your life needs special attention. There is no need to conform to the order in which the book is laid out. If you prefer to digest its content before completing the exercises, I encourage you to absorb the ideas, stories, and insights in a way that provides the most positive experience for you.

For those who want to go deeper into the subjects discussed, a bibliography of resources is provided for your review.

Our ultimate goal is to bring focus to what you want for your life and provide the knowledge, tools, and inspiration to bring it to fruition. Together we will ensure your mark matters. I am honored to be walking this path with you.

The Eagle was growing older. He felt it, accepted it, and even embraced it. But his vision was clear and his wings still powerful and strong. As he soared above the peaks, the valleys, and rivers below, the Eagle felt very much alive. Yet deep down something was different. A new passion was stirring in his soul.

The Eagle thought back to when he was first pushed out of the nest—so young, so much energy, so much fear, yet so much potential. Now the passages of his life had taught many lessons, and he felt called to pass on that wisdom.

He would teach the young to be bold and confident. He would help them to soar above their limitations. He would push them into a new world of possibility. And when they were ready he would give them the key to unlocking their dreams: "It is your spirit not your speed that leads you to be strong and free."

That would be his mark on the world.

It's Time to Soar

1

You are brilliant. It is your birthright as a member of the human family. Brilliance has many forms...

The same year this book is finished I shall celebrate my seventieth birthday. I certainly can no longer deny being in 'geezer' territory, but like so many of my generation, I don't feel seventy. The memories of surfing the beaches of Australia as a young man and the places I have lived all over the world are still vivid in my mind. A failed attempt to surf in Hawaii on a recent vacation, however, did remind me that the body ain't what it used to be.

One delightful compensation for my age is the role I now play of being a grandfather. I experience wonder and fascination being with the little people, who are the products of big people, who were once the little people I helped into the world.

I am also not encumbered by parental responsibilities and am free to savor and enjoy the evolution of personality and individuality. There is more time just to observe. These observations lead to seeing more clearly the pure joy, the scrumptiousness, and the brilliance of each child.

Each of us is brilliant. You are brilliant. Brilliance is your birthright as a member of the human family. Brilliance has many forms, and if your light has diminished and is not as bright as you wish, you have the ability to bring it to full power. That is why we are working together. But where do we begin?

An assessment of how you see yourself today is a good place to start. Pause for a moment and answer these questions.

What are three of your gifts and talents?

_____

_____

_____

What have you achieved in your life that you are most proud of?

_____

_____

_____

What mistake or failure has disappointed or disturbed you the most?

_____

_____

_____

It is perfectly understandable if you were unprepared to explore questions such as these so quickly. In fact, you might ask if there's a preexisting flight plan you could use to soar to new heights of achievement. Unfortunately, that's not the way it works. Reflection, assessment, and choosing a direction for your life are essential components in your preparation to soar.

Several studies of older adults found one of their most common regrets was that they spent so little time in reflection. The failure to reflect, to consider the impact of choices and decisions made with little thought, or somewhat unconsciously, had led to circumstances that were difficult and unwise. Many suggested they led lives that were dictated and directed by others. Only later did they realize they could have chosen more fulfilling and rewarding paths.

You are the author of your life...

This is a powerful lesson for those of you who are in the early stages of your lives and careers. The sooner you come to the realization that you are the author of your own life, the sooner you will begin to experience the life you imagine for yourself.

Take a moment to consider the first two questions. How easy were they for you to answer? If you have spent little time thinking about your life (Who am I? What do I want?) they may have been difficult to answer. Often a mixture of modesty, taking one's talents for granted, or just a lack of reflection leads us to undervalue our strengths, what we have achieved, and what we bring to our relationships, our jobs, and our community.

As I observe my grandchildren, I witness the uniqueness of each individual and marvel that we are all gifted with natural talents. If you are reading this book you have also developed skills and expertise and internalized a body of valuable knowledge and experience, both professionally and personally. When these are aligned and focused towards what you want for your life, you have a powerful recipe for making a lasting mark on the world.

In Chapter 4 we will bring even greater focus to this discussion by clarifying what will be defined as your *attributes*. These attributes are the combination of your attitudes, talents, skills, and experiences. They are your wings for soaring to new realms of possibility.

The last question (What mistake or failure has disappointed or disturbed you the most?) may have produced some discomfort. There are very few of us who can look back on our lives without a degree of sadness and sorrow about behaviors and choices that certainly did not serve our own well-being and may have hurt others. These regrets may vary in breadth and depth, but the comfort I bring you is that mistakes and failures are an integral part of the human journey.

What has transpired in our lives matters to the extent of how it has shaped who we are today. Have we learned? Have we grown? This cannot be emphasized more strongly. The past is not recoverable. We must let it go. Is that easy? Not at all. But the possibilities for our future are connected to the understanding that course correction—the realization we are heading in the wrong direction—will be an experience we have several, if not many, times in our lives.

The past contains two primary benefits: *good memories*—those that bring you pleasure as you recollect the circumstances of the time; and *wisdom*—the lessons you gained from the not so good memories.

Let me share one of my own most important lessons.

As a young man, I was driven to succeed. Success at that time was measured primarily in financial terms. In my mid-twenties I was already running a business in England that was owned by a U.S. company. I had a substantial income that allowed luxury automobiles, a beautiful home, and an elite lifestyle. It was very seductive.

At a point in time, the parent company got into financial difficulty and was unable to continue to provide the capital that our business needed. I was told that I could do whatever I wanted with the business since the problems in the U.S. were insurmountable.

As several colleagues and I believed our products were very viable, we decided to start a new business with a similar name, and we would own the business outright. This was perfectly legal, but we needed funding. My own financial resources were deployed to keep us going whilst we looked for other investors.

Our efforts to raise money were largely unsuccessful, except for one individual—a distributor for our products—who took the information we told him about the potential for the future and invested what was for him a significant amount of money. It was not enough. Soon the well ran dry, and his money and all of mine was gone.

Feeling completely defeated I returned to Australia. My wife and I had just had our first child, a daughter, and yet our spirits could not have been lower. We were back where our dreams had started but now were shattered.

Within days of my return, my problems were compounded. I was served papers from an attorney who represented the distributor who had invested in the company. He was suing me for misrepresenting its true financial condition. I was appalled. Did this person not know that I had lost everything in this company? It felt absurd.

This is where the lesson begins. I was so incapable of believing that I could have done anything wrong, I went against the best advice of my own attorneys and decided to fight the case rather than settle out of court, which they had strongly recommended. Two years later, confident in my position, I went to London to do battle in the courts.

I lost.

In his summary at the end of several strenuous days, the presiding judge made a statement that is forever seared in my mind: "I have found in favor of the plaintiff. This was a more difficult case than I expected. I believe the defendant to be primarily an honest man, however the evidence suggests that the issue is not the information he provided the plaintiff about the company, but more what he did not provide. I believe that if the plaintiff had access to this other information he may have chosen not to invest."

The judge awarded the distributor not only the full value of his investment, but also interest that would have accumulated on that investment and his attorney's fees. It was a sizeable sum, and added to that were my own costs. My financial hole had now gotten much deeper.

Incredibly, this did not cure my self-righteousness. Justice had clearly not been served. With no resources, I would obviously need to work out a payment plan. I was determined to negotiate the bare minimum. How unfair could life be?

Four years went by, and I had begun to recover personally and professionally. I had started a new business, was enjoying success, and my confidence had returned; however, the payment plan to my 'adversary' remained the same.

During this same time an uncle of mine began his journey of recovery from alcoholism. Whilst visiting with him one day he said, "David, I know you don't have a drinking problem, but I would like to invite you to one of my AA (Alcoholics Anonymous) meetings so that you can understand why it has changed my life." To support and encourage my uncle, I agreed. Little did I know that a seed was being sown that would change my life.

The meeting had an enormous effect on me. The vulnerability and honesty of the people involved moved me at the deepest level. At the end of the meeting I was handed a pamphlet which detailed the AA creed—*The Twelve Steps*.

I would describe them as a process for reconciliation, forgiveness, restitution, and the importance of living one day at a time. Today, people all over the world have embraced *The Twelve Steps* as they endeavor to recover from many different forms of addiction.

One evening, not long after attending that meeting, I discovered the pamphlet, still unread, on the side table next to my bed. Out of curiosity I began to peruse it. It is not my intention to take you through all twelve steps as the fourth and eighth steps are most relevant to this story. The fourth step states: "Made a searching and fearless moral inventory of ourselves."

I was immediately confronted by memories of my day in court, the judge's verdict, and my ongoing resistance to that verdict. I realized I had been self-deluding. Believing, as the judge had said, that I was fundamentally an honest person, it was too difficult to believe I had done anything dishonest. But I had.

Does the truth set you free?

Ironically, I had always considered integrity to be one of my highest values. Clearly a confrontation with a lack of integrity had now begun. Amazingly, however, I began to experience a sense of relief. Does the truth set you free? For me, now that I was no longer in denial, a burden was unquestionably being lifted.

The eighth step states: "Made a list of all persons we had harmed, and became willing to make amends to them all." Propelled by the revelation of my culpability and finally accepting responsibility for my actions, I immediately contacted the lawyers who represented the distributor. I asked for the amount still outstanding. Fortunately, my resources were at a point where I could settle the debt in full.

Every action has a consequence. Wherever possible, restitution needs to be made and responsibility taken. That is a sign of character. If we are wise, we also resolve to never make the same mistake again. I resolved to never again allow my quest for success to compromise my integrity. Having a clear conscience is a key ingredient for peace of mind.

A clear conscience is a key ingredient...

This experience led me to the belief that everyone deserves the opportunity for rehabilitation. Many of the greatest and most positive contributions to the world have come from those whose previous behavior had damaged society in some way.

In other words, many saints have sinned.

Jeannie Seeley-Smith, President and CEO of Perspectives, a not-for-profit agency in St. Louis Park, Minnesota, provides an inspiring example of the ability to transform our lives:

"Shirley Shumate worked in one of most depressing environments possible—a prison. Having the knowledge one is locked up without rights, affection, or emotional support, robs the soul of its dignity and the mind of its dreams—a hell on earth. So, for Shirley, a chemical dependency counselor, to daily walk the halls of a woman's prison and not only avoid succumbing to its overwhelming despair, but also bring hope to those incarcerated, was an amazing feat.

What was even more remarkable, Shirley inspired a community to share her vision of creating a place of solace and healing for those whom many would label derelicts. Such was the beginning of the Perspectives Supportive Housing Program which today has provided over two thousand women and four thousand children with a safe place to heal and begin again. Seventy-five percent of these women have rehabilitated their lives and become contributing members of society—an extraordinary achievement!

I look back to the day that Shirley shared her vision with me and others. Her contagious enthusiasm led us to a new realm of possibilities. Her belief that a completely broken life could be rebuilt provided the incentive. And her tireless drive to become the program's first director built the foundation to where it is today—the largest therapeutic, supportive housing program for recovering women and their children in the Midwest.

Shirley's compassion for society's 'throwaways' left this indelible mark on my life: a belief that all good work begins with passion and vision, and through totally committing to that vision, the right people are attracted to bring it to fruition."

"I look only to the good qualities of men," stated Mahatma Gandhi. "Not being faultless myself, I won't presume to probe into the faults of others."

Admitting mistakes, being ruthlessly honest with ourselves, and coming to terms with our failures is often very painful. The consequences of our behavior could have led to great difficulty for both self and others. This means that letting go of the past and forgiving ourselves can be tough. We may need to seek the professional help of a therapist or counselor—a route that was very beneficial to me.

Redemption inspires transformation.

Making amends, however, is not easy, for we cannot change what has transpired. It is gone. But it is an essential and courageous act. We learn that it is redemption that inspires transformation.

Some, of course, have little to be forgiven for, but no matter whether the weight of what we have experienced is light or heavy, let us ensure the future is not encumbered by a backpack of regrets. As we spread our wings, let us carry with us only our 'good qualities,' as we soar towards the life we truly desire.

"It is never too late
To start all over again
To feel again
To love again
To hope again.
It is never too late
To alter my world
Not by magic incantations
But by opening myself
To curative forces buried within
The powers of my self."

Rabbi Harold M. Schulweis

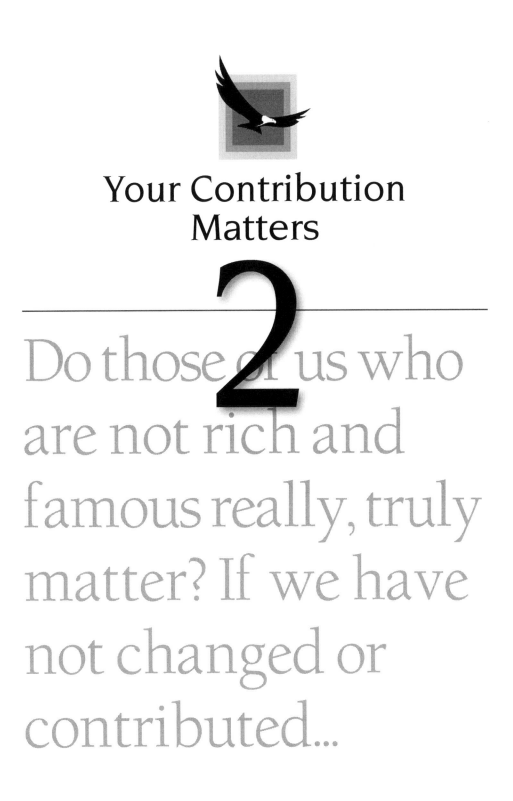

Your Contribution Matters

2

Do those of us who are not rich and famous really, truly matter? If we have not changed or contributed...

I subscribe to the Sunday edition of the *New York Times*. One of my favorite segments is the obituary column because it consistently astonishes me. I discover people of whom I have no prior knowledge, but who have achieved amazing things and contributed significantly to human progress.

Steve Jobs, the co-founder of Apple, stated: "I want to put a ding in the universe." Whilst that may appear beyond the aspirations of most people, it is, in fact, a desire of many.

This is where we often face a conundrum. Do those of us who are not rich or famous really matter? If we have not changed or contributed to the world like Nelson Mandela, or Bono, or Mother Teresa, or Oprah, or the many other humanitarians, artists, and leaders who are passionate about improving the human experience, is there any real significance to our existence? Where will be the evidence that we were even alive apart from a notation on a gravestone?

At my church we have an outreach called the Dignity Center. The center caters to people who are often homeless and struggling, yet have made a commitment to doing everything they can to live a life of self-sufficiency and dignity. What they need is not only encouragement, but also the resources and practical support to get back on their feet.

Every day volunteers such as lawyers, accountants, carpenters, caterers, engineers, counselors, government workers, ministers, college students, and many others with varying degrees of expertise, show up to provide the guidance and direction the 'clients' need. The results are inspiring. I have learned that homeless is not synonymous with hopeless.

I am fortunate to be the father of five children. In 2003, their mother and my wife of thirty-three years died of ovarian cancer. Jo was a joyful, loving person and full of fun. To this day friends of my children describe how they loved to come to our home, and at Jo's funeral some of them shared surprising stories of how troubles in their own homes left them looking for a haven.

Unbeknown to me at the time, Jo's welcoming attitude and warmth put them at ease and brought them comfort. An Australian by birth, Jo had instilled in our home many of the rituals of her heritage. One was afternoon tea with scones, cream, and lots of jam. Straight from school, the kids would come to the house and sit around the table where Jo would pour from a special teapot into proper cups and saucers.

Although Jo was essentially from a blue-collar family, for these kids it was as if they were having tea with royalty.

Did Jo's life matter?

To me, her children, their friends, our friends, and the numerous people over the years who knew her, the measurement of how much she mattered is how much she is missed. Her legacy lives in all of us. It can be summed up in the words of a close friend who said, "I never ended a conversation with Jo without feeling better."

"I have had the great fortune to meet many wonderful and inspiring people during my seventy-three years, but the most indelible mark was made by my mother. She was my teacher in third grade but died close to my eleventh birthday. Many called her a 'wise soul.' She taught me to think critically and encouraged me to always try to understand the other person's point of view— how the class bully was often just a frightened, mistreated child. Perhaps, however, the most poignant moment was on my ninth birthday. My dad was out of work, and we had little money. That meant a short afternoon birthday party around the dining room table with my brother, twin sisters, and three neighbors about my age. All we could afford was two, six-ounce bottles of ginger ale which was split seven ways and two cupcakes which were quartered.

Afterwards, I went to my mother and told her what a great birthday I had. She started to cry, hugged me, and said, 'You received so little and could have been disappointed, but you chose to be happy.' Then she said, 'Don't ever forget this day. Always remember… you make your own happiness.' Her words have become a mantra for my life."

Allen Shoup – CEO, Long Shadows Vintners

You matter. Your mark matters.

Every ding matters. You matter. Your mark matters. Use this knowledge, or belief, or understanding as that compelling reason to get up in the morning to face the challenges of this world and create the life you want. Look up, not down. The brilliance of the stars and the cosmos cannot be experienced by staring at the ground. Feel a sense of privilege that this universe is your playground.

My father instilled this attitude and approach to life into his three sons from the day we were born. Dad was the second of ten children born into a poor Scottish family. By age nine he was working to provide financial support. His daily routine was getting up at five a.m. and heading to work at a bakery. At eight a.m. he would head off to school where before long he was asleep at his desk.

At age thirteen he enrolled in the British Merchant Navy and spent the next seven years of his life transporting supplies all over the world. During this time World War Two broke out, and this meant his life was constantly in danger; in fact, one of the ships he served on was hit by a German torpedo but fortunately managed to limp into port.

There comes a time in our lives when we must make a critical choice: will we be a victim or a victor? My father decided that he would not let the circumstances into which he was born define who he was or what he could achieve. Whilst others made excuses, blamed others, or wallowed in self-pity, Dad made bold and courageous decisions.

After my parents married they decided to live in my mother's hometown, London. At thirty years of age, tired of the cold, smog, and pollution of that old city, they decided to emigrate to Australia. I was nine at the time, and my brother, Steve, was nearly two. Our final destination, Adelaide, was described to us as a picturesque land of continuous sunshine and endless beaches. And it was.

Despite that picture, the life of an immigrant is tough. A similar scenario is played out in any place called "A land of opportunity."

My father's work life in Australia began as a bartender and ended as a very successful realtor. Professionally he achieved more than any of the wildest dreams he may have had as a child in Scotland.

At some point—and I am unsure of the catalyst—he developed a profound gratefulness for how his life had turned out. Although my own perspective was that he had truly earned and deserved all that he had accomplished, my father's mentality was that he was extremely fortunate and blessed.

This deep sense of gratitude was transformed into a commitment to giving back, to helping those who he regarded as less fortunate. His passion was for those who had physical disabilities that severely limited their mobility. My father's work in this arena spanned over fifty years. It earned him recognition by the Queen of England and being honored as the longest serving volunteer in the history of his home state—South Australia.

People who leave their mark...

People who leave their mark on the world have a sense of purpose. Through these stories we learn how every contribution matters. It is also wise not to judge what contributions are more important than others. There are many needs in all sectors of society and in every corner of the world.

Whereas the media may give attention to what might be deemed more "noble" or selfless pursuits, my experience suggests that a well-run business which operates ethically, which is conscious of the imprint it is making, where employees feel safe and cared for, where they have the opportunity to provide for their families and secure their retirement, is a powerful contributor to a better world.

A sense of purpose is connected to a belief that we were created for a reason. For many people that belief is inspired by their religious or faith oriented upbringing. Within the tenets of the faith is the importance of doing "good works." Others experience a sense of purpose through seeing what needs to exist in their communities or in the larger world and are led to the question: What can I do to help?

"Ed Saugestad, who was my hockey and football coach at Augsburg College from 1967-1971, made an indelible mark on my life. Ed was the MIAC (Minnesota Intercollegiate Athletic Conference) coach of the year six times and he coached 22 All American hockey players—I was honored to be his first. He also taught in the Health and Physical Education department.

When I entered College, I knew I could achieve athletic success, but I had no confidence that I could excel in academics and I didn't see a future outside of sports. Growing up, I never received the message that learning was important. Neither my mother, biological father or step-father graduated from high school, and no one in my family had gone to college. In turn, I rarely did homework before entering college.

Ed was the first person to tell me that I was smart. Ed said, 'I know you can succeed academically.' He kept after me to produce good grades so that I could stay eligible for sports at Augsburg. I can't tell you what a tremendous difference that made. His deep concern for me, and his other players as student athletes, changed my life. He set me on a path I wouldn't have found otherwise.

Ed is the person who kindled the fire in me. Most importantly, he instilled the intellectual confidence that allows me to feel comfortable relating with anyone: from the CEO of a Fortune 500 company to the founder of an important non-profit to George Lucas—all of whom have been my clients."

Corky Hall – CEO Stellus Consulting

Take a few minutes to reflect on the following questions:

Who is a hero to me? Why?

_____

_____

When do I most experience happiness and joy?

_____

_____

To what do I currently contribute that provides a high level of satisfaction?

_____

_____

What is an organization I admire? Why?

_____

_____

Your willingness to invest time on these questions is the evidence that you value your life and that you want it to count, to matter. Your answers guide you to that unique contribution—the special mark—that only you can make on the world.

Contribution is the magic word for understanding how to achieve what we want for our lives. If we want a successful career, we must discover ways to contribute to the success of those we work for and serve. If we seek rich relationships, we look to how we can contribute to enriching the lives of our loved ones, our friends, and our colleagues.

When I am asked to speak to college students, an inevitable question is: "How can I get a good job?" My counsel is very straightforward: "Keep in mind that no individual or organization wants to 'give' you a job, but there are many organizations looking for people who will contribute to their success. Your first task is to discover an organization to which you would make that level of commitment."

In the consulting work we do at my company, the starting point is always aligning the leaders, teams, and individuals to the purpose of the organization. That purpose, in turn, is the contribution the organization makes to those it serves. Serve well, and you will be rewarded well.

How can so simple a principle be so profound? And yet it is!

Serve well and you will be rewarded well.

21

What businesses have you used as a customer?—those that contribute value to you. What friendships or relationships mean the most to you?—those that contribute value in ways that are important to you. Who are the people who are universally most admired?—those who make the most of their lives and contribute to the betterment of all.

The difference between luck and good fortune is that the first is arbitrary and the latter a consequence of contribution.

Let's reflect on why you were hired for your current position. Your resumé may have been the catalyst for an interview. Your performance in the interview landed you the job, and the job has a description of what you are supposed to do. Now here is the challenge—job descriptions define tasks and responsibilities. They do not define purpose and contribution.

The ultimate purpose of any person working in any organization is to help it succeed. What might appear obvious, however, is not. Purpose is very rarely clearly defined. This quest for clarity of purpose requires answering the 'why' question. *Why* does the organization exist? *Why* does the team exist? *Why* is there a need for leaders? *Why* are you important to the organization?

Purpose is the source of inspiration...

All winning teams are aligned behind a common purpose. That purpose transforms people who experience work as a daily marathon into a relay team that knows when, where, and to whom to pass the baton. Purpose is the source of inspiration; it influences culture and guides actions. Clarity of purpose is witnessed in daily attitudes and behaviors. Purposeful people shine out and are committed to maximizing their contribution.

So how do you put your arms around or find focus for the contribution you want to make? Below is a list of purpose-oriented words combined with quotes to stimulate thought and reflection.

Take time to identify the **five** that truly resonate with you. It's possible that you relate to all of them, however the exercise is designed to help you connect to those that most motivate and inspire you. If there are others not identified feel free to add them.

CREATING OPPORTUNITY – *"You have brains in your head. You have feet in your shoes. You can steer yourself in any direction you choose."*
Dr. Seuss

COMMUNITY – *"Wherever we turn we can find a person who needs us."*
Albert Schweitzer

INSPIRING – *"There is no certainty; there is only adventure. Even the stars explode."*
Roberto Assagioli

TEACHING – *"By learning you will teach; by teaching you will understand."*
Latin Proverb

BUILDING SECURITY – *"The key to abundance is meeting limited circumstances with unlimited thoughts."*
Marianne Williamson

LEADING – *"The art of leadership is growing people to produce enduring value."*
Kevin Cashman

PROBLEM-SOLVING – *"The possibilities are endless once we decide to act and not react."*
George Bernard Shaw

COACHING – *"You get the best effort from others not by lighting a fire beneath them, but by building a fire within."*

    Bob Nelson

ARTISTIC EXPRESSION – *"All children are artists. The problem is how to remain an artist once they grow up."*

    Pablo Picasso

FACILITATING COMMUNICATION – *"If you change the way you look at things, the things you look at change."*

    Wayne Dyer

INNOVATING – "Even if you are on the right track, you will get run over if you just sit there."

    Will Rogers

PROTECTING NATURE – *"The Earth does not belong to us: we belong to the Earth."*

    Marlee Matlin

STRENGTHENING RELATIONSHIPS – *"I've learned that you shouldn't go through life with a catcher's mitt on both hands. You need to be able to throw something back."*

    Maya Angelou

HELPING – *"How wonderful it is that nobody need wait a single moment before starting to improve the world."*

    Anne Frank

CREATING – *"Imagination is stronger than knowledge. Knowledge is limited. Imagination encircles the world."*

    Albert Einstein

TEAM-BUILDING – *"If we did all things we were capable of doing, we would literally astound ourselves."*

    Thomas Edison

My five purpose priorities are:

_____

_____

_____

_____

_____

There is no greater gift you can give to yourself than defining a purpose, that inspiring reason, to enter the day empowered to make the contribution you have intentionally designed. When you live with purpose problems get solved, challenges are overcome, goals are achieved, and life is rich.

So now is the time to define a purpose that you can embrace and fulfill. You may choose to work on a Life Purpose, a Work Purpose, or both. Focus on whatever is most relevant in your life at this moment.

For your Life Purpose consider these questions:

What do you find inspiring?

_____

_____

_____

What is important work that needs to be done?

_____

_____

_____

What would *give your life meaning?*

_____

_____

_____

Your purpose priorities and your answers to these questions are your guide to how you will state your Life Purpose. Here are some examples from others:

"My purpose is to provide for my family, be a role model for my children and contribute to my community."

"My purpose is to create works of art that give expression to my unique gifts and talents."

"My purpose is to create economic opportunities for others."

"My purpose is to be a catalyst for healing and understanding in broken communities."

"My purpose is to be the best human being I can."

"My purpose is to help young people believe in themselves."

"My purpose is to use all of my abilities to improve the quality of life for others."

"My purpose is to continue to grow and learn."

"My purpose is to be a protector of the environment."

Take time now to define your Life Purpose. Be patient, and remember it can evolve, be refined, and change as you gain greater clarity and awareness about the contribution that you truly want to make.

My Purpose

_____

_____

Let us now focus on your purpose at work. As most of us spend so much time working, it would seem wise to ensure that in our professional lives we find fulfillment and meaning. Respond to/answer the following directions/questions..

Who are three primary beneficiaries of your contribution? (Consider all those whose own work is impacted by how you do yours—peers, colleagues, customers, leaders, etc.)

_____

_____

 What are three expectations these people have of you? (Consider not only your qualifications and competencies but also your attitudes and behaviors—how you show up every day.)

_____

_____

What do you offer to meet those expectations? Identify three. (Consider your gifts, talents, skills, expertise, knowledge, and wisdom.)

_____

_____

_____

Now look at your answers and reflect on the insights you have gained. From here it is time to combine your answers into a concise statement of your Work Purpose. Here are some examples of purpose statements from others:

Leader: *I inspire and bring out the best in my team through listening, encouraging, and consistently acknowledging their value to the organization.*

Customer Service Representative: *I meet the needs and solve the problems of my customers through my efficiency, enthusiasm, and creativity.*

Teacher: *I open children to their potential and uniqueness through encouragement, caring, and my ability to connect.*

Account Executive: *I use my enthusiasm and communication skills to present creative ideas that solve my customers' problems and help their businesses succeed.*

Nurse: *I am dedicated to improving the quality of healthcare through my expertise, commitment, and compassion.*

Engineer: *I ensure that the products we produce are safe and of superior quality. I do this through my attention to detail and commitment to the highest standards of excellence.*

Receptionist: I provide a warm and welcoming introduction to my organization through my caring attitude and desire to be of service.

Flight Attendant: I provide a safe, comfortable, and enjoyable flight experience. I achieve this by being warm, friendly, and helpful.

Take time now to define your purpose at work. Again, be patient, and remember it can be constantly refined as you gain greater clarity and awareness about the contribution that you truly want to make.

My Work Purpose:

_____

_____

_____

_____

Congratulations on your willingness to do this work.

Purpose has power. It transforms the mundane into the magnificent. Your purpose will inspire you, provide a clear focus for your day, and give you the courage to live the life you imagine for yourself. Your purpose is the ultimate expression of how you will leave your ding on the universe.

"When you are inspired by some great purpose...

Your mind transcends limitations.

Faculties and talents come alive.

You discover that you are a greater person

by far than you ever dreamed yourself to be."

Patanjali

One Day I'm Gonna!

3

An idea was sparked, someone believed, a commitment was made, actions were taken, and the idea became a reality.

You and I are participants in a story of endless creation.

Look around you. Most of what you see, use, and often take for granted at one time did not exist. The chair on which you sit, the lamp providing light, the organization you work for, the plane on which you travel, are all the results of thought transformed into substance.

An idea was sparked, someone believed, a commitment was made, actions were taken, and the idea became a reality.

Recently I saw a televised news segment of a woman celebrating her 114th birthday. Incredibly, she is on Facebook and Skypes regularly with her family. For perspective, when she was born no human being had ever flown. She lives in a full-time care facility that provides a level of care—medically, environmentally, and socially—that would have been a fantasy to elderly people when she was a young person.

The ideas, visions, and dedication of others throughout her lifetime have created the conditions in which she now lives. We often fail to appreciate how these wondrous discoveries have so positively affected our lives.

My eldest grandson, when he was thirteen, was pestering his mother to get him a mobile phone. She was resisting this request for what I agreed were valid parental reasons. One day he approached me and vented his frustrations: "Grandad, all of my friends have a mobile phone. What do you think?" I responded that I did believe he was a bit young, to which he indignantly exclaimed, "Well, how old were you when you got your first cell phone?"

After my laughter subsided, I replied, "Fifty!" My grandson had no idea or perspective that cell phones at one time did not exist.

Each of us is creating every day whether we are aware of it or not. We create how we present ourselves to others. We create our interactions with others. We create our attitudes towards work. We create our careers. We create our relationships. We create most of our experiences and often how we feel.

That you take responsibility for what you have created to this point in your life is critical as we move forward in our work together. It doesn't matter whether you are happy or unhappy with your creation. What matters is that you grasp the fundamental truth that, moving forward, you have the power to create what you want for your life.

...you have the power to create what you want for your life.

I'm fully aware that circumstances often seem to mock this approach. I have lived long enough, however, to be given concrete evidence of the following—some people are born into circumstances that provide unlimited opportunity, yet their lives can be described as barely surviving. Others are born into the most adverse circumstances imaginable, yet discover ways to thrive.

Life is complicated and often arduous. Grief and sadness are part of the human experience. Yet, joy, laughter, achievement, and love also define what it means to be human. Each of us must decide which experiences we want more of in our lives and what we are willing to do about it.

As a child, my life was a blend of circumstances. In the early days of living in Australia, my parents encountered the common immigrant struggle of being poor but ambitious; fortunately for me, they were not poor in spirit. Their decision to move to the other side of the world was motivated by a clear focus—to thrive!

When I look back I realize there was nothing of true importance that was lacking in my life. Would I have loved a fancy bike like the ones some of my friends rode? Of course, most kids would have that aspiration, but at that time, those luxuries were not possible for our family. The foundation on

which I have built my adult life, however, has been the nurturing, the love, the encouragement, and the all-important belief in myself that my parents instilled in me.

Have you ever said or thought, "One day I'm gonna..."? And then you think of an experience you would like to have, a place you would like to visit, a person you would like to meet, an accomplishment that would boost your self-image and be incredibly satisfying. How long are you willing to remain in that vague and nebulous world? When will you put a stake in the ground and declare, "I'm gonna!"?

When my wife died at age fifty-seven, there were still so many new experiences she had visualized for her life left incomplete. Together, however, we had already done so much. Jo loved to travel and would often accompany me when a speaking engagement took me to a place she had always wanted to visit, but with five children, our financial responsibilities were significant. Many times we asked if we could afford to do this.

I am sure that people who tend to be cautious would not have agreed with our decisions at the time, but do you think looking back I have any regrets? Those memories are irreplaceable. I am not proposing that anyone be financially foolish, but Jo's passing made me aware that there is a certain arrogance to believing that there is endless time to do the things we say we have always wanted to do.

This is a serious consideration for all of us. There is a lot at stake for living in a perpetual world of *One day I'm gonna.* What is the price we pay for not pursuing our dreams?

The starting point for creating what you want is to allow yourself to dream. This can be very challenging, especially if you have never been encouraged or empowered to envision the possibilities for your future. Perhaps your dreams have been shut down by a lack of past success, but it is critical that you courageously declare what you want for your life.

So what do you want to create?

Life provides few guarantees, but goals that are never set can never be achieved.

The following is an exercise to stimulate your dreams. Take time now to courageously set aside any self-imposed limitations and respond to the following questions:

Five years from now...

What would you like to be doing?

_____

_____

Where would you like to be living?

_____

_____

Where will you have been?

_____

_____

What accomplishment will you be most proud of?

_____

_____

How will you be feeling?

_____

_____

How will things be different from how they are today?

_____

_____

With your answers in mind, now ask yourself: if creating what I want in the next five years is possible, what would that take, and do I have sufficient desire for its accomplishment? Without a strong desire, you will lack the level of commitment necessary for fulfilling your dreams.

Commitment is what establishes the creative tension between your current reality and what you envision. Right now, go and find a rubber band. Hold the band in one hand. Let it just dangle. When we lack commitment in our lives, we hang around like that rubber band— we dangle. Life may not be bad, yet it is rarely exciting. We may not even be unhappy, yet that wonderful feeling that comes with learning, growing, and achieving eludes us.

Now take the rubber band and stretch it between your two hands. Feel the tension that you have created. Consider that

tension as representing on the one hand your current reality and the other hand your vision—the dreams you have begun to articulate. The tension reflects your commitment. Tension, however, always seeks resolution.

Many people avoid this tension by being unwilling to establish goals or discover ways to express their potential. They shy away from commitment often because of the fear of failure or the ironic comfort that comes from remaining a victim of circumstances. Those who are willing to commit release the tension by consistently and incrementally moving towards their dreams despite setbacks or obstacles along the way.

And there are always setbacks and obstacles. What makes human beings different from other species, however, is that we have a mind and a brain that allows conscious choices and decisions. Transcending obstacles, responding positively to circumstances beyond our control is the path of all those who have left a lasting mark on the world. What will you choose?

"When I carefully reflect upon the influential people in my life and who in particular stood out, I would name C. Theodore "Ted" Molen. We met when I was in the early stages of my career in the financial services industry and he was changing his. Ted was thirty years my senior so as I taught him about life insurance he taught me about life.

Ted's impact was based on what he was able to see in me and the vision he cast for me. He enabled me to dream big dreams and provided the counsel and wisdom that allowed me to turn those dreams into reality. He was fond of saying 'chart your course by the stars and not the light of the passing ships.'

Several of my pivotal early adult decisions were influenced by Ted and decades later, I am eternally grateful that he took an interest in helping this farm kid see and believe what was possible."

> Mike Haglin – Senior Executive, Financial Services Industry

Here is a personal experience of applying the process of creation...

Many people who discover that I am an established author make the remark, "One day I'm gonna write a book." My tongue-in-cheek response is: "Just remember it will take you more than one day."

There is, however, a major truth in that retort. After all, at one time I was embarking on writing my first book. When I began, my goal was to finish in a year. It took four. Why? Life happened—five children and their daily needs, work and its demands, investing the time to nurture a healthy marriage, and being involved in the community. So many other important priorities can get in the way of achieving a goal.

So much can distract from achieving a goal.

But I did have a very strong desire. Having a book published would, I believed, provide a wonderful sense of accomplishment. It would mean overcoming self-doubt and prove I had something worthwhile to say. A book would add to my credibility as a professional speaker and consultant—a strong motivation to persist through the times when my commitment was put to the test.

Much of that first book was written between four and six a.m., the only quiet period in our house. Often I was unable to do even that. The demands on my time were such that I would discover I had not written anything for a month, even two, but I kept the dream alive and would pick up where I left off and move forward.

At the beginning of the fourth year, I felt that finally I had a manuscript for which I was willing to seek feedback. It is a vulnerable time for any new author but invaluable in determining the quality and relevance of one's work. I began to provide copies to family and friends. There were many suggestions for improvement, but unanimously, they felt I had a book worth publishing. At least that was the opinion of those close to me.

I was to learn that the world of book publishing can be disheartening and even cruel.

Unlike many new authors, I had the good fortune to be represented by an established literary agent with entry into the largest publishing companies in New York. My manuscript was forwarded to several of them. The working title of the book at that time was: *Creating Your Future*.

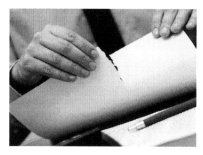

I received rejection after rejection after rejection. One letter my agent received from a well-known and respected editor said: "Based on your recommendation we were looking forward to reading David McNally's book. We have read it and believe there is not an original word in it. We are disappointed and have no interest."

It is at those times that one's commitment is truly challenged. The doubts seep in, the confidence diminishes, the energy depletes, and giving up on the dream seems a plausible choice. After all, surely these experienced editors must know quality writing, a story well told, and most importantly, what would appeal to the buying public.

I discovered that was not necessarily so.

My friends and colleagues who saw value in what I had written suggested that I put the book to a more stringent test than just having it read by people who knew me. They would help get the manuscript into the hands of executives and influential people all over the country. Those selected would have an interest in the subject matter, but, as I had no personal relationship with them, their feedback could be more candid and honest.

I loved that idea, and ultimately sixty copies of the manuscript were sent to a broad variety of people. The response was overwhelmingly positive and encouraging. Many generously provided suggestions that were incorporated into the final manuscript. What did these people see that the esteemed editors did not, and how would I continue to move forward?

There is a phenomenon that accompanies deep commitment. It is called synchronicity—a meaningful coincidence. My experience is that it often occurs when we are unsure and vulnerable and wondering whether or not to keep going. Then, wondrously, an encouraging connection, or meeting, or circumstance appears sending a clear message—don't give up.

...a phenomenon that accompanies deep commitment.

At that time a friend of mine, Rich Meiss, was the vice-president of a large company in the learning industry. Rich wanted to book me as a speaker for a conference scheduled about ten months away, but a criterion for the engagement was they only used published authors. I shared my situation with Rich, and we began to discuss the possibility of self-publishing.

Today, thousands of books are self-published. Back then, however, this was not as common. As an entrepreneur, the idea was not scary to me, and I had also been made aware that many famous and best-selling books had been rejected initially by numerous publishers. Perhaps, I thought, that could be my story too.

What tipped the scales in the decision was Rich stating that if I went ahead he would place an order for the first thousand books. I was stunned by his faith in me, and on a practical level, I realized that order would go a long way to offsetting what would be a considerable personal investment. The journey towards self-publication had begun.

It was not too long, however, before my commitment was severely tested again. I learned that another author had just released a book with the same title as mine—*Creating Your Future*. I was devastated since the brand I had been building through speeches, seminars, and workshops was aligned with that theme.

Extremely frustrated, I desperately searched for a new title. Nothing inspired me, and I got into the negative mindset of life being very unfair. But giving up was not an option, and because of my determination, another example of synchronicity presented itself.

During the years of their elementary education, my children attended a parochial school. One morning my youngest child Beth, a third grader, asked if I would come to school and attend the weekly Mass with her class. I protested that I had too much work to do, but her immediate retort was, "Dad you are always working." Motivated by guilt I soon found myself sitting in the pews of our church.

During the service my thoughts continually drifted. I was consumed by finding a new title for the book. For some seemingly disconnected reason my mind wandered to a conference I had attended a few months prior and specifically to a short animated film that had been featured. Called *To Try*

Again and Succeed, it was an inspiring story of a mother eagle encouraging her child towards the edge of the nest.

The eaglet was very resistant to this first attempt at flight, but its mother was determined to make it happen. As I recalled the beauty of the story I said to myself: "Isn't that interesting—even eagles need a push!"

EVEN EAGLES NEED A PUSH! The visceral response I felt was palpable. Is that it? Is that the new title? Was I being called to church to be given an extraordinary gift? Immediately following the service, I began to call my supporters to get their response to this potential title.

Overwhelmingly they loved it.

The energy around this new title was potent. Two friends, Sam Mancino and Stan Herman, owned a company in the advertising industry. A part of their core philosophy was defined as: "Happy to help a friend." That meant when a friend had a need but lacked sufficient financial resources, they would help in whatever way they could. They agreed to design the book.

The rejection I had encountered from the publishers stimulated Sam and Stan's competitive juices. They were determined that *Even Eagles Need a Push* would be designed like no other book on the market. It would be so distinctive that if you saw it in a bookstore, you couldn't help but pick it up.

Lisa Etziony, one of their leading graphic designers, was assigned to the project. Lisa did impeccable research into what made the look of a book appealing. Of course, the content of a book is what makes it successful ultimately, but first the buyer must be attracted to it.

Even Eagles Need a Push was released at the conference to which Rich Meiss had invited me to speak. Every participant received a copy. They were stunned by the beauty of the book. Published in hardback, the white cover featured the raised wing of an eagle. The typeface of the title was blue and gold. The interior was open and spacious, stimulating the reader to pause and reflect.

Looking back, I realize that none of the mainstream publishers would have designed a book such as the one my friend's creative genius had produced. I now know that if I had received a contract in those early days I would have been put into a production line of many other books without any input on design, and my book would have lacked any significant differentiation from the thousands of others in the publisher's catalog.

Even Eagles Need a Push was also an outstanding title. People gravitated to what it symbolized. People like television personality Larry King and Pat Riley, the famous basketball coach, endorsed it. I was moved by such a positive response. Within three months we had sold twenty thousand copies all by word of mouth. This felt extremely gratifying, and I was deeply grateful to all who had supported me throughout this journey.

But there is more to the story.

Because I knew that my literary agent had done the best he could to get me a contract, I decided to show him what we had produced. His eyes could not believe what he was seeing. He was so impressed that he asked permission to send this version of the book to the same publishers that had rejected the original manuscript.

As we were doing so well selling the book ourselves, I no longer needed the validation of a major publisher to prove the worthiness of my book. I was curious, however, to get their reaction and agreed to his request. I made one condition and that was the publishers would not be informed that they had already reviewed and rejected the original manuscript.

What followed was one of the most amazing weeks of my life. Copies of the book were sent on a Monday for delivery the next day. By Wednesday my agent was frantically calling me to say that three publishers had already declared their interest and were bidding against each other for the rights. By Friday I was in New York having lunch with a chief editor and his team from one of the largest publishing houses in the world, and he was offering me a six figure advance if I would agree to a contract.

Heady stuff, indeed. I called my wife, and she was incredulous. My agent informed me that the publisher's offer was extraordinary, an offer I shouldn't refuse. And I didn't. Here is the greatest irony. The publisher was the same one from whom I had received the debilitating rejection letter.

...being denied what we believe is good for us opens a portal...

So many times in our lives what in the short term appears negative, in the long term is positive. Perhaps a mistake or failure has turned into a powerful lesson. Maybe the pain of a relationship that didn't work out allowed us to discover the love of our lives. Often being denied what we believe is good for us opens a portal into what is truly best for us.

"In my senior year in high school, Mr. Maxwell, the assistant principal, told me to forget about college because he didn't believe I had the intellectual horsepower to succeed. I remember looking through my shattered ego and saying, half convincingly, "What's he talking about?"

The comment, however, lingered with me as Mr. Maxwell was one of the adults I most admired and the psychology teacher. If he felt this way, maybe it was true. That possibility was never far from the surface for years to follow. I did get into college studying fine art, but I remember thinking I was just an art student and not one with the ability to study math or science.

After two years, the Pygmalion effect was confirmed to be alive and well. My low grades convinced me to drop out. It would be another two and a half years before I confronted this subject again by returning to college. In the process of earning my degree (with a dual major in psychology and business) I had to complete a battery of assessments and then write an analysis of what this meant for my future. It was only then that I finally set aside the notion Mr. Maxwell had implanted in my mind.

Today, as I contemplate a diverse career, which has included graduate school, running companies, and being a coach to CEOs, I find myself reflecting back on Mr. Maxwell and smiling. As one of the most indelible driving forces in my life, were his words a calculated psychological ploy?"

Audie Dunham – Executive Coach and Artist

Now it is time to consider your commitment.

How do you put your arms around or find focus for the vision you want to create? Below is a list of vision-oriented words combined with quotes to stimulate thought and reflection. Take time to identify the five that truly resonate with you. It's possible that you relate to all of them, however the exercise is designed to help you connect to those that most motivate and inspire you. If there are others not identified feel free to add them.

Consider your commitment.

CHALLENGE - *"Screw it; let's just do it!"*
Richard Branson

MASTERING A SKILL - *"You have to fall in love with your work … You must dedicate your life to mastering your skill. That's the secret of success."*
Chef Jiro

LEADERSHIP - *"Yes leadership is about vision. But leadership is equally about creating a climate where the truth is heard and the brutal facts confronted."*
Jim Collins

HIGHER EDUCATION—*"The strength of a Curriculum Vitae is not about how good you could make it. It is about how good you can make it."*
Kenneth Obiakor

FAME - *"I've always been famous, it's just no one knew it yet."*
Lady Gaga

MENTORING - *"A mentor is someone who has been where you want to go and is willing to help you get there."*
Marcy Blochowiak

47

WEALTH – *"Wealth is not a matter of intelligence—it's a matter of inspiration."*
   Jim Rohn

RECREATION – *"When is the last time your computer restarted you? Don't forget about nature. Recreation means to re-create yourself."*
   Bryant McGill

TRAVEL – *"The world is a book and those who do not travel read only one page."*
   St. Augustine

POWER – *"When you doubt your power, you give power to your doubt."*
   Honore' de Balzac

ENTREPRENEURSHIP – *"Opportunities will come and go, but if you do nothing about them, so will you."*
   Richie Norton

SPIRITUAL GROWTH – *"Everyone is free to search for God in his own way and must himself make the effort to find that way for which he is seeking."*
   Joel Goldsmith

TALENT DEVELOPMENT – *"Our talents are the gift that God gives to us... What we make of our talents is our gift back to God."*
   Leo Buscaglia

CHANGE/VARIETY – *"Don't live the same year 75 times and call it a life."*
   Robin Sharma

VOLUNTEERING – *"If you're not reaching back to help anyone then you're not building a legacy."*
   Germany Kent

ADVENTURE – *"A ship in a harbor is safe, but that's not what ships are built for."*
    John A. Shedd

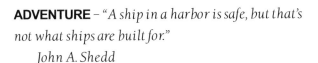

My five most important vision priorities are:

_____

_____

_____

_____

_____

With your priorities now identified let's leave the world of "One day I'm gonna," and take a stand on making your vision a reality. You have already ascertained what you would like life to look like five years from now so it is time to stretch that rubber band.

What will you do today that is a clear declaration of your commitment?

_____

_____

_____

What will you do in the next week to move towards your goals?

_____

_____

_____

In six months how will life be different than it is today?

_____

_____

_____

What do you want to have achieved in the next year?

_____

_____

_____

Reflect on your answers, and create a vision statement that represents how you want your life to look and feel. Here are some examples from others:

In the next five years I will have begun to fulfill my dream of traveling to other countries. My first trip will be to Italy as I am of Italian heritage.

In the next five years I will have been promoted to vice president and leading a division of my company.

In the next five years I will have completed my MBA. I will have been given greater responsibilities at work with commensurate financial rewards.

In the next year I will have skydived.

In the next three years I will be living in a new home and preparing to have a family.

In the next five years I will have written and published a book.

In the next two years I will have begun my life as an entrepreneur.

In the next six months I will be participating in and committed to a consistent fitness routine.

In the next five years I will be free of debt and building a sound financial future.

In the next two years my dream of playing the piano will become a reality.

In the next year I will be continuing my education and experiencing a high level of satisfaction from what I am learning.

My Vision

_____

_____

_____

_____

Take a moment now to reflect on the vision you have established and what it will mean for your life to be moving towards this vision every day. Celebrate that you have taken charge and become responsible for how you want to experience your life. And if there is one insight or piece of wisdom to embrace immediately, it is this—life is about experiences. A memorable life is one that is full of memorable experiences, and you are now on your way to creating them.

A rich life is full of rich experiences.

"Don't ask what the world needs.

Ask what makes you come alive.

What the world needs is more people who have come alive!"

Howard Thurman

Rich Relationships
Rich Life

4

Can you count on them? Do you trust them? Do they challenge you? Do they have your back?

This book is interwoven with stories people have shared about those who have significantly influenced their lives in the most positive ways. Fulfilling our purpose and realizing our vision is rarely accomplished without the encouragement, collaboration, and help of others. We now enter the all-important domain of relationships.

The quality of our lives has a direct connection to the quality of our relationships. Love, acceptance, affection, joy, recognition, job satisfaction, praise, progress, support, laughter, fun times, and high on my list, meaningful conversations... all this and much more are dependent on human interaction.

Can you count on them?

Think of a relationship you highly value. How does this person affect your life? Can you count on them? Do you trust them? Are they enjoyable to be with? Do they both compliment and complement you? Do they challenge you? What would your world be like without them?

It is often said, especially in a marriage, that relationships need to be fifty/fifty or, put in another way, an equal split of compromise and contribution. That begs the question: who is measuring the fifty?

When a relationship is deep and enduring, the commitment is total—100 percent. Each person knows that the other wants the absolute best for them. Each wants success, happiness, and fulfillment for the other. In difficult times each is walking the same path, empathizing, sympathizing, supporting, and encouraging. As a result, the relationship is rich because of the positive contribution each is making to the other.

As we go through life we experience many forms of relationships. Our family and friends provide a substantial portion of the more important relationships. Work, however, introduces us to many other relationships, some of which are brief and transitory. Some are contentious and unpleasant, and others—the rich ones—inspire us to learn and grow.

A key factor in your success, both personally and professionally, will be your ability to build the kind of relationships where trust, respect, and even admiration describe how people perceive and feel about you. In a work environment, exceptional qualifications and expertise can be rendered ineffective when an individual is unable to build strong relationships.

How then are rich relationships created?

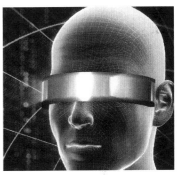

People cannot see inside of us. They react to what they see and observe. While intentions are important, it is our demeanor and actions by which others assess and judge us. As my friend, I appreciate you meant to call me. That you called in my time of need meant the world to me. Your action was the evidence you cared. As my boss, it is nice to know you feel I'm an important member of the team. I don't know, however, unless you tell or recognize me.

I had the privilege several years ago of co-authoring a book with Karl Speak called *Be Your Own Brand*. It has become a bestseller and is available in at least a dozen languages. The book reveals that brands are not about fancy packaging, elegant logos, or creative advertising. Brands are, in fact, about relationships. With companies and their products or services that we buy time and time again, a strong relationship has clearly been established.

Here's how it works. At one time we had our first experience with the product or service, which became a strong brand for us. Because that experience was good, perhaps even exceptional, we had an incentive for a second experience. If the second experience was a repeat of the first, there was little hesitancy in going back for a third, and so on. Each experience built on the other, and the impressions made on our minds catalyzed positive feelings inside.

This same pattern is present within our own professional and personal relationships. Every interaction with another person leaves an impression. The sum of those impressions is the perception we have of another, which translates into how we feel about them. Most importantly, the impressions we make on others affects their perception of us. This is your "personal brand."

To build a strong corporate brand a company must deliver on its promises. That same commitment applies to the building of strong personal brands.. Once again, it is not our intentions but our actions that determine how we are perceived and branded.

Intentions ▸ Actions ▸ Impressions ▸ = Brand

In our consulting practice, we work with several of the world's most successful companies to ensure their brand strategies are implemented throughout every level and with every person in the organization. Our services include developing strong, effective leaders. We define the purpose of a leader as: *to engage others in committing their energies and expertise to achieve the shared mission and goals of the organization.*

A title does not determine a leader. The evidence is in whether he or she has followers. 'Followership' is directly connected to relationship. People follow leaders they believe in, leaders who have their team's best interests at heart and prove it with their actions. The questions we always start with in our leadership development sessions are: "Are you the kind of person others want to follow? Or, why would people want to follow you?"

These questions are the catalyst for an important understanding. We cannot change others, only ourselves. Being an effective leader, therefore, is not about learning what to do to others—it is about learning what we can *be* for others so that they trust us and are inspired to follow.

"As a head and neck surgeon at the Mayo Clinic for the past forty years, I have been fortunate to have many superb teachers. By combining the best aspects of my mentors, I refined and developed my own surgical technique. The lessons from my elders were many, but one from Dr. Kenneth Devine has again and again served me well.

Dr. Devine was a superb surgeon and one of daring, innovation, and tremendous experience. His operations combined speed from no wasted steps with almost 'bloodless' surgery, yet were secondary to his great knowledge of anatomy and tumor behavior. He was an excellent clinician, a caring doctor widely acknowledged as a world class physician. One of his lessons to me was his approach to adversity. He handled crises, chaos, and the unexpected with a calm patience combined with absolute control.

During difficult surgical operations there can be times of life-threatening events. As the 'captain of the ship,' the surgeon needs situational awareness, skill, and experience to effectively deal with such challenging situations. To do so by never raising your voice, nor criticizing a team member, remaining calm and in control, allows the entire team to function much better. The lesson—never lose your cool!"

Kerry D. Olsen, M.D.

Whether we are in a designated leadership position or not, the way we lead our lives determines whether we attract people who admire, trust, and even love us. By raising our awareness of how our behavior affects others, both positively and negatively, we access the power to manage the perceptions they have of us. We are taking charge of our personal brands and, thus, the depth and quality of our relationships.

Let's address a common concern people have in this discussion about personal brand: "Do I have to pretend to be and project someone I'm not?" Definitely not! Strong brands are authentic—they are not false or phony.

We cannot avoid being branded. An investment of time and effort in exploring how the quality of our relationships influences the quality of our lives, and being willing to examine how we *show up* in the world, will be truly invaluable. It will reveal how often, through our interactions with others, we leave our own imprint, or mark, on the world.

This is not an exercise, however, in endeavoring to be all things to all people. That would be unhealthy and could even lead to a level of paranoia. Your efforts clearly need to be focused on those with whom a rich relationship serves you both professionally and personally.

When we consider some of the strong, well-known personal brands in the world, both past and present, such as Martin Luther King Jr., Adele, Alicia Keys, Muhammad Ali, Richard Branson, Maya Angelou, Bill Gates, Ellen DeGeneres, and others, we realize that our values may or may not align with theirs. In other words, we can't be all things to all people, and that's not what we're striving for. Our goal is to build stronger and deeper relationships with those who matter to us.

To help you gain clarity around your personal brand, we will follow a process and model my company, TransForm Corporation, uses in working with clients.

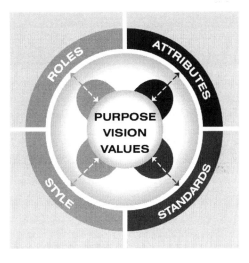

The perimeter of the model defines your Brand Presence. Your *Presence* is what others can visibly see or observe about you. It cannot be emphasized enough that other's perception is determined by behavior. Your *Presence* encompasses the roles you play, the attributes you bring to those roles, the standards you establish, and your style, both physically and interpersonally.

The center of the model is the core of your personal brand, which is your Brand Essence. Your Essence is invisible to others, but it is what drives your brand. What people see on the outside reflects what's happening on the inside. Strong brands, both personal and corporate, are motivated and inspired by a sense of purpose, a clear vision, and guiding values.

59

We will now invest some time in reflecting on the strength of your personal brand, not only where it might be currently, but also where you aspire it to be.

As this exercise evolves, a picture of all the components of your personal brand will emerge. Whilst you may share some characteristics with others, the final combination will distinguish your brand from any other. Let us begin.

Roles: No matter who we are there are certain roles we play in our everyday lives. There are our professional roles at work and personal roles with family and friends. A leader in an organization suggests roles such as coach, mentor, guide, team builder, and motivator. Personal roles may include parent, spouse, son or daughter, friend, volunteer, and the many others, such as caregiver, that maybe unplanned but are shoes we choose to fill.

Take a few minutes to identify the roles you play every day.

What are your five most important personal roles?

_____

_____

_____

_____

_____

What are your five most important professional roles?

_____

_____

_____

_____

Of course, you will observe that many others share similar roles. It is not the roles, therefore, that determine the quality of our relationships; it is how we deliver on those roles. In every role we play others will have expectations. Do we meet or exceed those expectations, or do we miss the mark?

Attributes: I wrote in Chapter 1 that each of us was born with natural gifts, and over the years we have built new skills, developed expertise, internalized a body of knowledge, and gained wisdom from our experiences both professionally and personally. Put all of this together, and you have an incredible recipe for contributing to others and building meaningful, productive relationships.

To maximize your attributes, you first need to know what they are. Often, as you have already discovered, it is simply a lack of reflection and assessment that leads to being unaware of our attributes and how they contribute to the building of our brands.

As you answer the following questions, don't be modest or compare yourself to others. This isn't about anyone but you, and no one will see your answers unless you choose to reveal them. Some examples from others are provided. If you find yourself struggling, however, seek out one or more trusted friends who know you well and ask them to assist you.

What particular knowledge and experience am I known for? List at least four. (Examples: creativity and design; business development, following through, and thinking strategically.)

What are things I know how to do well? List at least four. (Examples: project management, communication, facilitation, and work effectively with teams.)

What are some of my special abilities? List at least four. (Examples: connecting with people, creating value, enjoying life, and adapting to different situations.)

Now reflect on what you have identified that can be attributed to you. Give thanks for the gifts you were born with, and give credit to yourself for what you have earned and learned over the years. Now let's discover how to leverage those attributes for even greater success.

Standards: We all know people who stand out because of their insistence upon maintaining high standards. Our standards—how well we fulfill our roles—impress or fail to impress others. At work do we aspire to excellence and to exceed expectations, or are we content with good enough? At home, or with family and friends, do we purposefully seek to understand and meet their needs, or do we give little thought to what they want and value?

If our everyday actions make impressions on others, then others are impressed when we have high standards. When a company has high standards for customer service, we see it, we experience it, we benefit from it, and we love it. When we model high standards for our family and friends they get to witness excellence in action.

Examples of personal standards

- Punctuality
- Keeping promises
- Flexibility
- Being positive
- Honesty

Examples of professional standards

- Being prepared for meetings
- Timely response to e-mails
- Listening to understand

· Adaptability

· Inclusiveness

Take some time to identify some of your standards.

In your personal life what are the five standards to which you most aspire?

_____

_____

_____

_____

_____

In your professional life what are the five standards to which you most aspire?

_____

_____

_____

_____

_____

You'll notice that we used the word "aspire" when asking these questions. This is intended to not only motivate us to soar higher, but also to deal with the reality that certain circumstances or conditions can, at times, prevent us from meeting the standards we seek. Deadlines, emergencies, competing priorities, urgent demands, illness, can all effect the quality of our work or our ability to meet the needs of our families. At such times we need to be realistic with our standards to protect both our own and others' sanity.

Style: The way we dress, our grooming, the way we hold ourselves, our bearing or posture, all contribute to impressions we make on others. There is a reason that the business of coaching job applicants is booming. How we show up visually is, rightly or wrongly, how others begin to judge how competent and qualified we might be for the position. Whilst we may get a second chance at a first impression, why take the risk?

Interpersonally we also have a style—different ways of interacting with others. For example, some people are outgoing, and others are more reserved. Some people talk readily, while others tend to listen more. Of course, there are also blends and extremes in any of these ways of behaving. There is no best style, but we do need to be aware of how interpersonally we are perceived.

Take a look at the accompanying chart and select the five behaviors that best reflect your style. When complete, consider how long you may have been this way. Most often we realize that our style was set when we were very young. If you have children their different "styles" will validate this observation.

Identifying My Style

Review the following descriptors of your interpersonal style, and identify five style characteristics that best reflect your behavior. (If you have other descriptors you would like to use, add them to the list below.)

STYLE CHARACTERISTICS	
❑ Adaptable	❑ Open-minded
❑ Agreeable	❑ Optimistic
❑ Assertive	❑ Organized
❑ Creative	❑ Perfectionist
❑ Confident	❑ Persistent
❑ Compassionate	❑ Persuasive
❑ Cautious	❑ Practical
❑ Decisive	❑ Precise
❑ Determined	❑ Quiet
❑ Dependable	❑ Reliable
❑ Effective	❑ Resilient
❑ Efficient	❑ Spontaneous
❑ Empathetic	❑ Serious
❑ Enthusiastic	❑ Thoughtful
❑ Even-tempered	❑ Team player
❑ Flexible	❑ Warm
❑ Friendly	❑
❑ Helpful	❑
❑ Independent	❑
❑ Intense	❑

The interpersonal component of your style is not a predictor of success or whether or not an individual is perceived as a strong brand. The determining factor is a component called *versatility*. Versatility is the ability to adapt to changing interpersonal circumstances. For example, are you respectively assertive when one's opinion needs to be heard, or do you listen attentively when other points of view need to be respected?

Always, always, always remember that people cannot see inside us. They are always reacting to our behavior. We build our personal brands one impression at a time, and it is our actions that determine the perception others have of us. Personal brands become strong when others witness consistent behaviors that express confidence and competence and are considerate, inclusive, and trustworthy.

...people cannot see inside of us.

"Edwina (Winnie) Gilbert was the person who left the most indelible mark on my professional life. Winnie was the first major airline female senior executive in America and perhaps the world. She was a remarkable woman, and I am privileged she took me under her wing.

Despite only a high school education, Winnie occupied the boardroom with the famous Apollo astronaut Frank Borman, a very traditional command and control executive. Winnie tells of her first executive meeting when Col. Borman asked her to fetch some coffee. She responded, "Frank, you're a big boy, get up and get it yourself." As a woman executive in the 1970s, this was a courageous yet calculated risk to level the playing field. Borman was so impressed with Winnie that he cited her in his autobiography.

Winnie recognized my potential early on. She took me to leadership meetings with simple instructions: watch, listen, learn. She was an absolute master at determining competing interests and assessing different management styles to achieve desired results. Not only did I learn a lot, they became part of my own mentoring repertoire.

At one time, I made a career decision mistake. Winnie knew this, but let me go. The job was one for which I had no enthusiasm. A lesson learned. Do what you love. When the time came to rescue me, Winnie provided an exciting new opportunity. It was clearly aligned with my skills and interests. The legacy from Winnie's patience, insight, and support has been to pass that understanding along to those I have led over the years."

Peter Wilander – Chief Commercial Officer, Gate Group

Building a strong brand takes effort and energy. So why would you want to make such a commitment? One answer ties back to the purpose of this chapter, enabling you to build quality relationships. A second and equally powerful answer lies at the core of a brand, and that is its *essence.* Your essence is who you perceive yourself to be as evidenced by what you want your life to be about, what you want to create, and what you believe.

Specifically, your Brand Essence is comprised of your Purpose, Vision, and Values (see previous model). The good news is that you have already worked on and defined your purpose and vision. It is this desire to live a full and authentic life that will motivate and inspire you to have the highest standards in delivering on your roles, to fully use your attributes, and to have a style that demonstrates versatility in meeting the needs of others.

Let's now bring your Purpose and Vision back into focus.
Go back to chapters 2 and 3 and write them again here:

My Purpose

_____

_____

_____

_____

_____

My Vision

_____

_____

_____

_____

To complete your brand essence, we now need to identify the values that are most important to you. Your values are the principles by which you live your life. Your values affect not only what you think and feel but also how you behave.

Integrity is the integration of our values with our actions. Your sense of self, the esteem in which you hold yourself, is clearly connected to your commitment to your values. One of the key reasons people leave companies is the lack of alignment between their values and that of their employer. When core values clash, any relationship suffers.

Below is a list of sixteen values combined with quotes to stimulate thought and reflection. Take time to identify those that most resonate with you. It is possible that you relate to all of them, however the exercise is to select five that would be your most important. If there is a value or values that are not on the list, feel free to add them.

66 **INTEGRITY** – *"If you don't stick to your values when they're being tested, they're not values: They're hobbies."*
Jon Stewart

INDEPENDENCE – *"If you want your life to be a magnificent story, then begin by realizing you are the author."*
 Mark Houlahant

GENEROSITY – *"Friendship isn't a big thing – it's a million little things."*
 Author Unknown

ECONOMIC SECURITY – *"What people need first is economic security, and only when they have that can they afford to focus on human rights."*
 Peter Munk

COOPERATION – *"Every human interaction offers you the chance to make things better or to make things worse."*
 Barbara Brown Taylor

COMPETITION – *"I'm not in competition with anybody but myself. My goal is to beat my last performance."*
 Celine Dion

LIFE BALANCE – *"Be yourself. Everyone else is already taken."*
 Oscar Wilde

70

FAIRNESS – *"Live so that when your children think of fairness, caring, and integrity, they think of you."*
  H. Jackson Brown Jr.

INFLUENCE – *"A good head and a good heart are always a formidable combination."*
  Nelson Mandela

EXCITEMENT – *"Who's to say tomorrow won't be the best day of your life?"*
  Matty Healy

ACHIEVEMENT – *"The future belongs to those who believe in the beauty of their dreams."*
  Eleanor Roosevelt

FUN/PLEASURE – *"I just got one last thing….spend each day with some laughter….get your emotions going."*
  Jim Valvano

INNER HARMONY – *"Yesterday I was clever, so I wanted to change the world. Today I am wise, so I am changing myself."*
  Rumi

LEARNING – *"Be willing to be a beginner every single morning."*
  Meister Eckhart

FAMILY – *"Call it a clan, call it a network, call it a tribe, call it a family. Whatever you call it, whoever you are, you need one."*
  Jane Howard

PERSONAL GROWTH – *"If you keep telling the same, sad small story, you will keep living the same sad, small life."*
  Jean Houston

My five most important values are:

_____

_____

_____

_____

The experience of our consulting team in working with people to build strong personal brands is that answering the questions you have just completed is an experience many have never had before. The busyness of our lives somehow prevents us from addressing critical questions that pertain to the business of life, but unless we pause and reflect, how do we correct?

We have one more lap to run—developing an action plan for building a stronger personal brand. Answer these questions:

Do you feel that you have room for growth with regard to building deep and enduring relationships? Why?

_____

_____

_____

What would be the payoff personally and professionally for having stronger relationships?

_____

_____

_____

Where do you feel inhibited in your ability to strengthen current relationships or build new relationships?

_____

_____

_____

How do, or could, others benefit from being in a relationship with you?

_____

_____

_____

Select a **role** where you could clearly make a greater impact and define how.

_____

_____

_____

What **attribute** do you need to no longer take for granted and how could you use it more effectively?

_____

_____

_____

What is one **standard** that affects your colleagues or family the most that you could improve?

_____

_____

_____

What component of your **style** has the most appeal and why?

_____

_____

_____

Now list four actions that you believe will strengthen the perception of your brand.

_____

_____

_____

_____

Well done. This work requires a level of commitment few are willing to undertake. Clearly, however, you are determined to leave no stone unturned, and the payoff will be significant.

There are many ways to make your mark on the world, but few will have greater impact than how others experience you on a day-to-day basis. The ripple effect of who we are and the relationships we nurture and nourish extends throughout generations.

A smile, a word of encouragement, an honest discussion, taking time to listen, caring, a sense of humor, raising aspirations, high standards, giving recognition, being aware, accountability, and sensitivity are all behaviors that define the best in humanity. And they have never been more in demand and needed than they are today!

"Your beliefs become your thoughts,
Your thoughts become your words,
Your words become your actions,
Your actions become your habits,
Your habits become your values,
Your values become your destiny."

   —Mahatma Gandhi

Soaring Above Adversity

To provide people and organizations with the knowledge, skills, and inspiration to perform at their best.

In his best-selling book, *The Road Less Traveled*, M. Scott Peck begins the first chapter with these three words: "Life is difficult!" I was much younger when I first read that statement and can clearly recall feeling it was somewhat depressing. I saw myself as a positive thinker who could determine what would and would not happen in my life. In other words, I had a lot of chutzpah but little wisdom

This touch of arrogance may have been connected to the fact that, since my mid-twenties, I had been an avid reader of self-help books in all their guises and had participated in numerous seminars oriented towards taking charge of one's life. So passionate am I about human potential that it has been my profession for forty years. My own work purpose statement is: to provide people and organizations with the knowledge, skills, and inspiration to perform at their best.

Having experienced so much in my life and now, hopefully, much wiser, I believe that positive thinking is misunderstood. One misinterpretation is that thinking positive thoughts will prevent having to face anything difficult. The facts prove otherwise. Examine the lives of people who have left a significant mark on the world, and you will witness stories of how each has confronted and overcome formidable problems and numerous difficulties.

Examine the lives of people...

Life has clearly brought me in touch with this reality, and so I now believe a better interpretation of positive thinking is 'positional thinking.' How we choose to frame what happens in our lives is what proves most useful. Adversity, for example, is then judged as neither foe nor friend.

This mindset is of the utmost importance. The accomplishment of the wonderful work we have done so far in defining your purpose, clarifying your vision, and developing a strategy for building rich relationships, all rest on your commitment to staying the course and soaring above the challenges that will inevitably come your way.

Adversity is neither foe nor friend.

Take a moment to consider a situation or event in your life that was very difficult.

Describe what happened.

_____

_____

_____

_____

How did you first react to this situation?

_____

_____

_____

_____

Has the situation now resolved itself? If so, why or how?

_____

_____

_____

_____

What have your learned from this experience?

_____

_____

_____

_____

As you reflect on your answers, the insight that will best serve you is that whenever we are confronted with adversity we are faced with choices. Do we intend to be a victim or a victor? Will we meet resistance with resilience? Will we accept the current reality but not give up on the future? Will the prospect of defeat be no match for the strength of our determination?

Here is a story from my own life in which I assure you I had to summon all my positive thinking in order to emerge triumphant.

One evening in November 2010, I was scheduled on a flight to England from my home in Minnesota. My purpose was to visit a close friend who had been diagnosed with esophageal cancer, and the prognosis was not good. I was determined to offer my support and to ensure we spent time together should his life now be coming to an end—this was fortuitous as he passed away several months after my visit.

A few hours before the flight I was having a haircut. The barber, Tod Leaf, whom I had been going to for nearly thirty years, noticed a lump on the back of my neck just below my left ear. As he guided my hand, I felt a small 'egg' rising out of my skin. The lump was so prominent that we were both astounded it had escaped my attention.

I felt a small "egg" rising out of my skin.

Although feeling unsettled, I decided to wait until after visiting my friend—a week later— before having the lump examined. My doctor was concerned by what he saw and immediately organized an appointment with an ear, nose, and throat surgeon. The lump was a tumor, and a biopsy revealed it was a malignant cancer: squamous cell carcinoma. "That lump needs to get out of there as soon as possible," the surgeon said emphatically.

Like so many people who have virtually escaped any major illness throughout their lives, I was stunned and left facing so many questions, not only about the surgeon's sense of urgency, but also about the implications for my family, my work, and the future I had envisioned for my life.

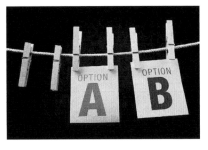

My wife's experience with ovarian cancer had taught me how important it is to take charge of one's own health and medical treatment. I decided, therefore, that getting a second and third opinion on my situation would help me choose the best course of action.

Going into extensive detail about the process of choosing my medical team is unnecessary here, except to say that I found my research extremely valuable. The treatment of cancer has made considerable advances in recent years, yet some institutions are clearly more progressive than others.

The choice for my surgery was the Mayo Clinic in Rochester, Minnesota. There were three factors that influenced my decision: the reputations of the institution, the surgeon, and the demeanor of the surgeon himself—an excellent example of a strong personal brand!

No matter who you are or what you have accomplished in life, receiving a diagnosis of cancer means you will probably never feel more vulnerable. Having someone who would empathize and cater to that vulnerability was very important to me. Now that may not be a priority for everyone, but it was certainly a reflection of my personal need—technical competence combined with a great bedside manner.

The Surgery

The operation to remove what was found to be a very large tumor was extensive. The two hours planned took seven. The cancer had spread to lymph nodes and was about to wrap itself around my carotid artery. The operation was described by the surgeon as one of the most demanding of his career. The good news was that he and his team removed all the visible cancer, and a PET scan found no other trace in my body.

As insurance, however, a program of radiation and chemotherapy was recommended. This was to begin approximately a month later when my body had healed sufficiently from the surgery, and I had the strength to handle what was to come.

The treatment entailed seven weeks of daily radiation, excluding weekends. Interspersed during that period were three sessions of chemotherapy. It was rugged, arduous, and debilitating, a common experience for all those who have had a similar diagnosis. My ability to withstand this regimen of daily "poisoning," according to the physicians, was due to my good physical condition leading into the treatment.

Throughout the ordeal, I deliberately held back on trying to interpret what all of this meant. In the middle of extreme nausea, the last thing you need from others, although they mean well, are philosophical platitudes.

The approach I took might be described as somewhat 'Buddhist': stay in the moment, no matter how unpleasant, and observe what happens. Not an easy task, I assure you.

Stay in the moment.

As the distance has grown from this "life is difficult" experience, I have several observations:

Lesson One: Responding to Crisis

When faced with a crisis we typically respond in several ways:

Denial: figuratively burying our heads in the sand, hoping it's a bad dream, and we'll wake up to discover the problem had disappeared.

Resistance: getting angry and fighting reality in a futile effort to turn back the clock or maintain the status quo.

Acceptance: whilst unhappy, or sad, or even puzzled by a situation, we are willing to deal with the truth, no matter how severe.

Early in my career, I produced an inspirational film about Terry Fox, a young Canadian who, at the age of eighteen, lost his right leg to cancer. If you are unfamiliar with Terry, he is now regarded as one of Canada's greatest heroes.

At the time of his diagnosis Terry was understandably in shock and disbelief. What captured my imagination about Terry's story was his ultimate response to what had happened. He invested little time in denial and resistance. His attitude was summed up in these words: "If this is the way I have to go through life, I'll make the most of it." And indeed he did.

He would commit to a much larger goal.

After three years of rehabilitation, Terry committed himself to what would be called "The Marathon of Hope." Terry was a dedicated athlete despite the loss of his leg and had even completed a marathon, but now he would embrace a much larger goal: to run the entire width of Canada and raise a million dollars for cancer research.

Terry never made it across Canada as the cancer metastasized to his lungs, but he did complete 3,339 miles of the journey, and the final tally for cancer research was twenty-four million dollars. Terry died within a year, but the mark this introverted young man left is astounding. Today the foundation established in his name has raised over 750 million dollars through its annual Marathon of Hope runs throughout the world.

It is much easier to write about heroes than to be one, even if the heroism is directed exclusively at oneself. But, here I was, many years after producing a film about Terry, reflecting on his response and endeavoring to apply it to my own life.

Fortunately, I quickly realized there was nothing to be gained from denying and resisting my reality. The victim stance of "why me" I knew would only add more emotional pain. Having already lost my wife to cancer, I was able to accept "why not me!" Acceptance, I felt, would promote a greater sense of calm and a more positive "wait and see" attitude. That is the space I decided to occupy.

That is the space I decided to occupy.

Lesson Two: I Am Enough

From the moment my cancer diagnosis became public, the support and encouragement I received from family and friends was incredible. Calls, e-mails, texts, and cards came every day from people I barely knew or could not remember that I knew. This kindness enabled me to peek into people's hearts and souls and see how they came from a place of genuine compassion and caring.

Like so many people, I can easily fall into the trap of feeling that I am not 'good enough.' For whatever reason, another book, more money in the bank, a more prestigious title, would be the signal that I had finally made it. The experts, ones who claim to understand the motivation for these strivings, tell us that we are seeking the feeling that we are okay, that we are loveable.

If they are right, then my experience with cancer, and all that it wrought on my life, brought profound blessings.

I realized I was truly loved.

Despite my many mistakes and failures, my successes and accomplishments, my idiosyncrasies, or any other form of behavior my grandchildren might describe as "weird," I now know, unequivocally, that I am truly loved.

In other words, another achievement, a better title, or more awards change nothing that is truly important. According to all the wonderful people who reached out with their support, I'm good enough as I am.

And so are you!

Lesson Three: Patience

Ten weeks after finishing radiation and chemotherapy, according to the medical team, my recovery was going well. To me the process was frustratingly slow. I kept asking, "When will I feel normal?"

Clearly, I was being reminded of what was both within and outside of my control. My body, after all, had literally been attacked and poisoned for seven weeks. The good blood cells were destroyed along with the bad ones. An internal tsunami had taken place, and there was a lot of repairing and healing to do.

I was beginning to be productive, but the naps to refresh my energy were much more frequent. Was that, however, a bad thing? This slower pace led to my being more observant and appreciative. In the middle of a delicious snooze, I was often gifted with a creative idea. If others experienced the same thing, perhaps this would lead to a new movement—Snoozers Anonymous! The first step: I am powerless over my naps!

My friends told me I looked well, for which I was thankful, but I was still forty pounds lighter than normal, and I longed to return to a more robust look and the energy that accompanied it. I was told that goal may take a year or longer to reach.

So, in accepting that reality, the word that describes how I began to manage my life is *patience*. It is truly a transformative word.

Patience is truly a transformative word.

To be patient is to let go of artificial, self-imposed timelines. Being patient allows others to be themselves and not be judged by rules and expectations not of their own making. Having patience means maintaining equanimity in the midst of traffic jams. When we are patient, a flight delay is not regarded as a personal affront. Patience, in fact, is the most realistic and healthy way to deal with the unfolding of our daily lives.

I began to ask: "Who am I to say what should happen in the next moment, the next day, or week, or month?" Patience is that virtue that teaches us no matter how life surprises us, the good and not so good, we have the ability, the capacity, and the spirit to handle it.

Lesson Four: Live Boldly

Around the four-month mark of my rehabilitation, I knew the prognosis for a complete recovery was good. Week to week I was getting stronger, and there was every reason to be optimistic that I would live for many more years, but something inside of me was insisting, "Don't take any chances!" Let me explain.

Don't take any chances!

After seventy years on this planet, there's something about which I'm convinced: you and I are not here to mark time—we are here to make our mark! There is a force, a spirit, within each of us consistently bursting to express itself. It implies much more than completing a bucket list. It is about the desire to be immersed in the life-giving process of creation, to experience daily the joy of being engaged in living boldly. George Bernard Shaw stated: "I want to be thoroughly used up when I die... I rejoice in life for its own sake."

We are here to make our mark.

My desire for you is that you will embrace those words and resolve not to take your life for granted. Together, let us be bold in finding ways, every day, to go above and beyond the call of duty, to provide exceptional value and service to those we work with and for.

Let us be bold in expressing our love and appreciation to those who give meaning to our lives, and let us boldly make plans for experiencing everything we declared we would do on our "One day I'm gonna" list.

Take a moment now to pause and consider your answers to the questions at the beginning of this chapter. Is it possible that you have a different perspective about the situation than when you were immersed in it? My wish is that you learned much from your experience and realize that you are now a stronger, wiser, and more resilient human being.

That is how I have come to assess my confrontation with cancer. This assessment, however, was enabled by one of the most incredible experiences of my life.

Here is how it happened.

THE MASK: A Symbol of Transformation

As I have suggested, when faced with a life-threatening situation, it is the rare person who can look beyond his or her immediate survival and give thought to the notion that this experience could eventually be transformative. As should be, the focus is on the moment, enabling all energies to be channeled in the direction of the challenge.

Clearly that was my perspective as I went through the seven weeks of radiation and chemotherapy.

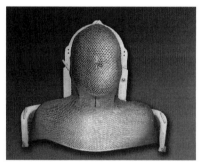

Radiation treatment is dangerous. To ensure the radiation was focused on the area of the head and neck where the cancer cells were active, the technicians in the department of radiology molded a plastic 'mask' that fully covered my head and the top of my shoulders. The mask was used every day of treatment, which for me totaled thirty-five days.

To most people the mask has an ominous look since it has bolts on the side that screw into the table upon which one lies. The intention is to restrict head movement as there are so many areas where one wrong move could mean a permanent and significant disability. For example, as a professional speaker, damage to my vocal chords would be devastating.

The radiation itself is not painful, but side effects I still live with are loss of taste, lack of saliva, and compromised hearing. The good news is that today my overall sense of well-being is excellent. I am productive and fully engaged with my family, my friends, and my work.

As you might imagine, the mask does not hold pleasant memories for me. Although I am very appreciative for the breakthroughs that have been made in curing cancer, it never occurred to me that anything positive would ever come from being in the embrace of that mask for so long.

Someone else, however, saw the mask in a totally different way and had a vision for its use that I could never have imagined.

The fourth of my five children, Jessie, is an artist who I am pleased to say is getting increasing recognition for her distinctive work. On one of the trips to the hospital for treatment, Jessie was my driver. She took advantage of the opportunity to observe what I was experiencing, but on the way home enquired as to what happens to the mask once the treatment is over.

Now, if you have artistic children, or know artists, or you yourself are an artist, then it should be completely clear that artists' brains explore worlds where there are no limits. This especially applies to Jessie, who, once she discovered that the hospital threw the masks away, wasted no time in making claim to it.

There is a truism, at least for me, that suggests parents should never ask their older children questions if there is a risk you may not like the answers, so my only counsel to Jessie was the following: "I have no idea what you are going to do with the mask, but know one thing—I never want to see it again."

As the months went by, the quest to regain my health and strength absorbed all my physical, mental, and spiritual resources. What Jessie might be doing with the mask, quite frankly, never entered my mind. Then one night, eight months after my treatment, a fundamental shift in how I perceived my cancer experience took place.

The St. Paul Art Crawl is an annual fall event where Jessie joins many other artists who feature their work. As any proud father would do, I always make Jessie's space my first stop. This year, upon entering the room, I was drawn immediately to a piece hanging on the far wall.

My eyes could not make out exactly what it was, but my visceral response was so great that I knew it was the mask. I crossed the room very slowly with my emotions running rampant, but as the image came into full view, I was confronted not with my past, but my future.

...its eyes peering into my soul.

On the wall—its eyes peering into my soul—was a glorious eagle!

I stood there for several minutes as I endeavored to absorb the symbolism of this magnificent work of art, and then I read Jessie's words on a plaque framed next to the eagle.

"I believe that we all have totems that guide us through our lives. For my father, it is the eagle. It is a symbol of his spirit, vision, and strength. I've made this work from my father's radiation mask. This mask represents his enormous spirit, his vision of a healthy and cancer free life, and his unfaltering strength."

92

Even those whose purpose it is to encourage others face times when they themselves need to be encouraged. At that precise moment, as I stared back into the eyes of that eagle, I became fully aware that my spirit did not feel enormous, nor did I have a vision for a cancer free life, nor was my strength unfaltering. I was, instead, in a state of significant uncertainty and unclear about what even the day ahead might hold.

But here was a precious daughter letting the world know how she perceived her father and what she wanted for his life.

And that was all I needed.

Ah, how limiting our thoughts can be. Oh, what restrictions we place on what could be. Thank you, thank you, thank you Jessie for your imagination that transformed the ominous into the magnificent.

"We are all beautiful... However, we may not know or believe this. We may be mixing up arbitrary physical qualities with divine inheritances that need our recognition. Let's be clear—let's recognize all that we have going for us. Let's live the beautiful lives that are ours to live."

—Reverend Margaret Stortz

Consciously Creating
Amazement

6

In other words, if
we haven't learned
and grown we have
been merely existing.
Leaving our mark on
the world requires ...

If age, as we all hope, does bring wisdom, then it is unquestionable that the need for purpose, the need for vision, the need for rich and enduring relationships, and the ability to soar above adversity, applies in some form no matter how old we are. Add to that list the need to develop an attitude of appreciation for all that is truly amazing in our world.

I use the word amazing purposefully as a wake-up call to examine where we are focusing our mental energy, what we are taking for granted, and what we are missing as we walk or, perhaps, run along the path of our lives.

Several years ago, I was in a taxi heading to a hotel in New Jersey where the next day I was to be the keynote speaker at a conference. Taxis are often driven by the most intelligent,

engaging people if one only chooses to connect. How we got into this conversation I cannot recall, but what the driver said was truly a gift: "You know, we have lost our sense of wonder. There are so many amazing things happening in this world every day, but we let them pass on by—we have no perspective on how incredible they are."

I remembered this interaction after a friend confided that after his mother's passing his father spent an unusual amount of time following the news on television. What began as an escape from grief rapidly descended into cynicism. "The world is going to hell in a handbasket," became this man's mantra.

The taxi driver and my friend's father provide two vastly different views of the world. Our views or perspectives shape how we show up in the world and the imprint we ultimately leave: whether we live boldly, as suggested in the last chapter, or live in fear; whether we have a deep sense of gratitude or take things for granted; whether our attitudes are positive or negative. All is influenced by the lens through which we look at what is happening in the larger world and in the smaller world in which we operate daily.

They shape the mark...

Ironically, how we get our news today is nothing short of amazing. Within minutes what is happening on any part of our planet is beamed into our living rooms. A little more than a century ago a war could have begun and ended before people in other countries had even heard about it. Today, tragedies, conflicts, and disasters are presented to us at the press of a button.

Let me be clear. I want to be informed and aware of what is going on in the world, but I refuse to be weighed down by what is beyond my control. We are generally oblivious to what damages our psyche, and that is why the attitude with which we digest the news is critical. Consider that the news is the news because it is the exception to the norm. How we frame and balance the news, therefore, with the incredibleness that surrounds us, is the key to experiencing amazement.

This perspective enables us to accept the negative reality of world events but not be consumed by it, for there is another positive reality. In every country, in hundreds of cities, on every part of the globe people are NOT participating in cynicism. They are having a different conversation: how do we create better lives for all? And, more importantly, they are taking action.

Recently I learned of a non-governmental organization (NGO) called Pencils of Promise. The genesis of this remarkable initiative begins with a young man, Adam Braun, who was inspired to build schools throughout the developing world. Where did the idea begin? From a simple answer to a question. At the age of twenty-one, while backpacking in India, Adam asked a little boy begging in the street, "What would you like most in the world?" The boy replied, "A pencil."

He replied: "A pencil."

Adam was stunned, but that one answer stirred his soul and eventually gave clarity to the purpose he sought. Pencils of Promise has now become the manifestation of his commitment to that purpose. It has gone beyond anything Adam could have envisioned. A new school is being built every one hundred hours, and thousands upon thousands of children, through access to education, are being awakened to their potential and given hope. Now that is amazing!

Sarah Owen Bigler, a mother of two, told the following story on Facebook. Bigler was waiting in line at a Target store near her home in Indiana. Eager to complete her transaction, she was held up by an elderly woman counting out her change to pay for her purchases. "Part of me, the part that had a long day at work, the part of me that had a one-and-a-half-year-old having a meltdown in the cart, was frustrated with this woman and the inconvenience she had placed on me," Bigler wrote.

"But then I watched this young employee, Ishmael Gilbert, count her change, ever so tenderly taking it from her shaking hands. I listened to him repeatedly saying, 'Yes, ma'am.'" Bigler said it was only when she realized her young children were closely watching the scene and learning a valuable lesson about patience and kindness... "that I realized I too needed a refresher on this lesson."

Ishmael, a father himself, responded, "It just feels good to be recognized for good work, but this isn't something new. I treat all customers the same—the way I want to be treated. It felt good because that's the kind of example I want to be for my daughter."

The number of people...

Adam Braun and Ishmael Gilbert are people whose stories are amazing in terms of the marks they are leaving on the world. Yet we become aware of and inspired by them through people like Sarah Owen Bigler, who grasped the significance of her experience and shared it on Facebook, a medium that has spread amazement all over the world. You can put different names to different causes to different circumstances, and they are being repeated every minute all over the planet. The number of people who are compassionate, kind, and good vastly exceeds those who are not.

"There have been so many incredible people who have inspired me, but it was one little seven-year-old who changed my mission in life. Daniel was one of the young children shot at Sandy Hook. He had this gorgeous gap-tooth smile and a mop of red hair. He reminded me of my son—Damian. That really hit home. When I saw his parents on television, I told my husband my life was about to take a big turn. I went from full-time mom and magazine contributor, to full-on gun safety advocate.

I started an organization—Evolve—to help promote more gun safety conversations in America. The gun world is very complicated, so the intent was to respect both sides of the issue and find ways to compromise. Little did I know what I was in for.

On this often lonely road, I learned you have to be relentless, thick-skinned, empathic, unreasonable and always be looking for the silver lining. I also discovered you need a lot of smart people with big hearts! During the bleak times, I always thought of Daniel..

There is no perfect ending here, but our organization has some of the most viewed gun safety commercials ever made. We were first to create much of the dialog that is currently part of the national narrative around gun safety. Without a little boy called Daniel—who got up for school one day, but never came home—I know for certain that I could not have tried to take on such an enormous task."

Rebecca Bond - Founder, Evolve

It has been said that the best things in life are free, but to grasp the significance and truth of those words requires us to pause and reflect upon how to use such simple wisdom. "Almost the entire world is asleep," says Tom Hanks in the movie *Joe vs. the Volcano.* "Those who are awake live in constant amazement."

The human body is amazing.

So, let us take a moment to see if we can break out of the cocoon of our daily lives and peer out into our amazing world.

Nature is amazing—the earth's structure, ecosystem, and its place in the universe will astound us if we stop to observe for a moment. Technology is amazing—consider that a mobile phone today has more capacity than the computers that took Apollo 11 to the moon. The human body is amazing—the immune system that enables us to recover from illness is incredible! Medicine is amazing—so many diseases have been eradicated that not long ago were deadly.

Love is amazing.

Air travel is amazing—within hours we can be in another country, experiencing a different culture and language. Movies and television are amazing—they inspire, entertain, and make us laugh. Music is amazing—we dance and we soar. Friendship is amazing—how wonderful to have someone who has our back. Love is amazing—there is no better feeling. It truly conquers all.

101

What is ultimately amazing is you. Yes, you! There are currently over seven billion people on the planet, and not one has a face like yours. Not one has the exact same blend of gifts and talents as you. Not one has had the same combination of experiences. Not one has the exact same thoughts. Your voice is unique. Your fingerprints belong to you alone. No one can express themselves or contribute to the world like you. The implications of this awareness can take one's breath away.

Take time now to identify what surrounds you that is amazing. If that seems a formidable task, let me rephrase the exercise: What do you take for granted? What is an integral part of your life every day to which you give little thought but which, in fact, through another lens is amazing.

In his book, *A Million Miles in a Thousand Years*, Donald Miller writes: "If you think about it, we get robbed of the mystery of being alive... because we don't remember how we got here. When you get born, you wake up slowly to everything. From birth to twenty-six, God is slowly turning on the lights, and you are groggy and pointing at things... The experience is so slow, you could easily come to believe that life isn't that big of a deal, that life isn't staggering. Life IS staggering, and we are just too used to it."

My friend, Bill Martin, who wrote *The Sage's Tao De Ching*, a book full of incredible wisdom, has a simple yet profound approach to each day: Show Up—Pay Attention—See What Happens. This is a clear call to be fully present, to be aware of all that surrounds us, and to be ready to be amazed.

"My father made the most indelible mark on my life. Born in 1914, into a working class family, Arthur Hauser grew up in St. Louis, Missouri. He graduated from Washington University with a degree in engineering, but his passion was music. He played several instruments and had a dance band in college. Musicians are often emotional people as music taps into our hearts and elicits deep feelings.

My father brought great energy and compassion into our family life. He was the connector, a hugger and an extrovert, always ready to love everyone, without exception. I distinctly remember overhearing a conversation between my parents. I must have been 7 or 8 years old. I don't remember the content but what I do remember was his attitude of possibility and optimism.

He was a man who believed the cup was always half full. I clearly remember thinking, 'I want to be like my father. He is happy and genuine and his soul is full of gratitude.'

This didn't help me escape sadness or tragedy. My parents, both aged 59, were killed in the world's largest airplane crash. It was in the Canary Islands and 587 people perished. I grieved for a very long time. What remains in my heart, however, is knowing that who I am today is a direct result of a man who showed me what a heartfelt, engaged life can look like. Here's to you Dad!"

Cheryl Hauser - Teacher

It is not easy to move from seeing the glass as half empty to perceiving it as half full. Our lives are filled with choruses of "Ain't it awful," and yes, the truth is that awful things do happen, and they happen to good people. What we witness is heartbreaking and often beyond comprehension. Putting our arms around the enormity of it all can feel overwhelming.

There is, however, another truth.

The world will not advance, and positive change will not happen if we align ourselves with the negative. Understanding the duality and ambiguity of human existence requires much thought and reflection, but with tragedy there is also triumph, with conflict there is reconciliation, with sadness there is joy. A fully lived life encompasses all of these feelings and experiences.

So how do we consciously create amazement in our lives? Here are three steps.

Take Charge of Your Thoughts

When I first wake up in the morning my thoughts are far from amazing. Like many, my mind quickly jumps to all that I must do—current business challenges, what the future might bring, and any family issues in which I may be involved. Many of these thoughts and concerns are just repeats in a different form, time, and place, that have endeavored to hold me in their grasp for most of my life.

I have learned that if I allow these thoughts to take control of my mind, then the result can be stress and anxiety, and that's before I've even left the bed!

Negative thoughts trigger negative feelings. As the quality of our lives is related to how we feel about life, then every day needs to begin by channeling our thoughts towards the positive feelings we want to experience. For me that means a powerful exercise, which directs my attention to the present moment and reminds me of what is real versus merely feared, what is within my control and what isn't, and what truly matters and what doesn't.

I am reminded of what matters.

I have been dedicated to a morning ritual for over thirty years. A quiet, peaceful environment is a necessity and, ideally, a thirty-minute commitment. As an early riser, I realize that this time frame can be challenging for those whose biorhythms are opposite to mine, but I can assure you that if you try this for a week the transformational, calming effect will be clearly noticeable.

My heritage dictates that the day starts with a cup of tea—English breakfast with a dash of milk. I take this to my favorite chair and light a candle. On the side table are books and magazines, the content of which is designed to descramble my thoughts and align them towards the positive and what I want to create for the day.

I begin by spending time in contemplation. Purposefully, I direct my mind to thoughts of gratitude. I reflect on the many blessings that are a part of my daily life. This ensures my focus is on what I have rather than what I don't have. I become clear that I may not have everything I want, but I have everything I need to fully embrace the potential that the day ahead presents.

I then move to reading as I drink my tea. The wisdom of others grounds me in the present and reminds me of life's possibilities and the magnificence that surrounds me. Thought by thought my self-imposed limitations dissolve, new vistas open, and my soul is stirred by the prospect of all that has yet to be learned, accomplished, and experienced.

There is no question that the ritual requires discipline and dedication. This means it must become a priority. When my five children were young my commitment was often tested. Most of us lead busy lives, and it is easy to allow our 'to do' list to take control of our day and our thoughts, but how much on that list leaves you with a sense of amazement? There is always time for what we deem to be truly important.

The ritual remained even when I experienced times of great difficulty, some of which I have written about. In fact, I needed it more than ever. In reading about the lives of others, one learns that our mutual journeys always include struggle, disappointment, and grief. For those who continue to show up and not give up, we learn that there are seasons to life. Just as winter turns to spring, and grey skies give way to blue, our lives are given fresh opportunities to shine, and buds of new beginnings emerge.

Just as winter turns to spring...

To my surprise and pleasure, I have discovered that my children, as they endeavor to respond to the pressures of careers and families, have also begun to employ a morning ritual to achieve a focused and resilient state of mind. As with many of their generation, however, much of their information comes via the wonders of technology. Sources of inspiration and encouragement are readily accessible on the Internet and the many apps available via mobile phones. The form doesn't matter—the ritual does.

While playing the great game of life, there is no more important workout than one that strengthens our optimism, gratitude, and resilience. The consistency of this workout, our willingness to practice daily the channeling of our thoughts, will ultimately determine whether we win or lose. I wish I could walk around in a natural state of amazement, but that is not my reality. I need my ritual as an invaluable reminder that if I stay awake, something amazing will present itself every day.

In the great game of life...

Take Charge of Your Words

The words we use communicate our thoughts and feelings. As with our thoughts, negative language produces negative feelings. Positive language stimulates positive feelings. In many studies of people who were brought up in homes where negative, even abusive, language was prevalent, it was discovered their lives were often defined by what they heard and the limitations those words placed on them.

If the proportion of negative words you use far outnumbers those that are positive, the possibility for experiencing amazement in your life will be significantly diminished.

Think about your feelings after an argument with a loved

one and how words used in anger hurt and sting. Now think about the opposite, being comforted by the words, "I love you." How does being criticized compare with being affirmed? What is our experience of being ignored or put down versus being acknowledged and encouraged?

So the question we must ask again is: how do you want to feel? If your answers include being peaceful, playful, motivated, and inspired, then let's explore how your language can help make those feelings your dominant reality.

"That's to live for."

There is a casualness to the words we use that are worth examining. "That's to die for," is a popular response to something desirable. What an irony! I'm not sure that dying just to experience a delicious dessert, for example, is the best of ideas. Of course, that may sound facetious. But stay with me. My wife, Jo, when she was battling cancer, changed the expression to match the intention: "That's to live for!" And isn't that what we truly mean? Test it out.

I work out at a health club near my home and am always impressed by the number of people of all ages who are committed to their wellness. From the young hard-bodies to those, like me, who wisely place a high value on staying healthy, we all move cautiously, yet somewhat harmoniously, among the weights and treadmills. Many

conversations take place, but I am intrigued by how many times I hear the question, "How are you?" met with, "Oh, I'm hanging in!"

Rephrased, those words appear to mean: "Oh, I'm surviving." Admittedly, when life throws out big challenges, merely surviving can be a courageous act. I assure you I was barely 'hanging in' when going through radiation and chemotherapy to treat my cancer. In fact, when people asked how I was doing, the only honest answer could be: "Bloody awful!"

There are also many ways that people communicate where the language is designed to make a simple connection. For example, "How are you doing?" in most instances means the same as "Good morning," for rarely are we looking for a thirty-minute, detailed revelation of what is going on in the other person's life.

The principle underlying this discussion is that we are not about surviving—we are about thriving! If you've reached this stage in the book, the evidence is clear that you are about flourishing, prospering, and leaving your mark on the world. In that quest, your language plays a critical role.

We are about thriving!

Next time someone asks, "How are you?" consider responding with: "Excellent" or "wonderful," or if those words are over the top for your personality, how about simply "good" or "really good." Now, if that is a major change in your behavior, be ready for people to look skeptically and say: "Wow, what have you been smoking?" Laugh it off, and stay with the experiment.

You may ask: "Are you suggesting 'Fake it 'til you make it?'" Not at all. The word 'fake' literally means not genuine, a forgery, an illicit copy. There is nothing fake about you. You are not a copy of anything. Your responses are a declaration of how you want to feel—how you want to show up in the world. Your language is a powerful tool for creating the person you intend to become.

Words can harm or words can heal. They are often used without understanding of their potential long-term effect. When I was growing up my mother would endeavor to comfort me with the idiom, "sticks and stones may break your bones, but words will never hurt you." Unfortunately, that was not the case for me, for I was very hurt by words hurled my way.

Consider the word *hate*. We hear people say, "I hate this food, I hate this weather, I hate those people, or I hate it when you do that." There is an energy that accompanies every word we use. Is the energy of *hate* and the feeling it produces what you want?

I am not suggesting that there are not people who easily stir negative feelings, nor that the weather, bad service, delays, poor communication, thoughtlessness, or a myriad of other things can be frustrating, but when hate is the word we unconsciously use to express how we feel, then those feelings will be magnified well beyond what these situations call for.

Experiment with replacing *hate* with *dislike*, and observe how your feelings soften and even subside.

Observe how your feelings soften.

How important is love in your life? By most measures it is one of the most amazing feelings one can experience. How often would you like to feel loved and loving? Then take note of how often you use the word love during your day. It is an expression of love to find opportunities to compliment rather than criticize. Encouragement, recognition, support, empathy, and listening are all the language of love.

Let us now examine the words we use on ourselves. "What a fool!" "Idiot!" "How dumb was that?" Very few of us have escaped making mistakes, doing foolish things, and making unwise choices. Beating ourselves up with negative language changes nothing to the good but always deepens our self-wounding, our unwanted feelings.

The prescription we are following here is simple: if the words you use provoke a reaction or feeling that you don't want, then remove those words from your vocabulary. Find substitutes that allow you to express your feelings without the negative energy behind them. Break out of the unconscious responses that have become your norm, and use the words that create the positive experience you desire.

Why not go to the extreme? Replace "I hate this weather" with "I easily forget how magical a rainstorm can be?" Once again—test it out.

Take time for the following exercise. In the left-hand column below write five words or phrases that you habitually use, but may not serve you. If you choose to, remove them from your day-to-day language. In the right-hand column write their replacements. Here are several examples.

I hate	I prefer
This is awful	This is challenging
I'm a fool	I'm human
I failed	I learned
I should	I will

_____   _____

_____   _____

_____   _____

_____   _____

I offer two words now that will make you smile or maybe suspicious, for you have undoubtedly heard others utter them before: "Trust me!"

Accentuate the positive.

New habits, the experts tell us, take a minimum of thirty days to form and take hold. So "Trust me" means that if you make a focused effort to transform your language for at least thirty days and "accentuate the positive and eliminate the negative" as the old Bing Crosby song suggests, your life will change because your feelings will change.

And how amazing is that?

Take Charge of Your Actions

Now here's a conundrum. In the bigger picture, despite what we have just discussed, we are neither our thoughts nor our feelings. Understanding this is one of the most important lessons of my life. Who and what we are transcends any thought or feeling we experience at any moment.

Our thoughts sweep in and out randomly. Our feelings are influenced by the situations in which we find ourselves, the events of our lives, and the quality of the relationships we develop. That we can choose how we act at any given moment, despite any erroneous thought or negative feeling, is what makes us human beings so amazing.

We can choose how we act.

In Chapter 4 we were reminded that people cannot see inside of us and that they judge us by our actions. We may have good intentions, but only action makes those intentions a reality. People can be impressed or unimpressed by how they observe our behavior on a day-to-day basis. With consistent, positive impressions you become, in others eyes, the kind of person they want to be in a relationship with or the leader they want to follow.

The most important person you need to impress, however, is yourself. This means acting with integrity when no one else is watching. It means keeping your promises and following through on your commitments. It means learning to be in control of yourself when the events of your life are out of control. It means staying calm and treating people with respect when you might feel that respect is the last thing they deserve.

One of the most influential books in my life has been the *Bhagavad Gita*. It is the foundation of the Hindu spiritual tradition and has been revered by people such as Ralph Waldo Emerson and Henry David Thoreau. It was in the reading of this text that I was introduced to the concept of "Right Action." I have since learned it is also a fundamental teaching of the Buddhist philosophy.

At the risk of oversimplifying this ancient masterpiece, Right Action is the commitment to our actions always being in alignment with what we know and believe to be right. Right Action takes account of the effect our actions have on others and prescribes that we never act in a way that would intentionally harm others.

In a world where lying, manipulating, and cheating are far too accepted and common, Right Action speaks to a supreme and higher standard for all of us. In the Stephen Mitchell translation of the *Bhagavad Gita*, we read: "Whatever a great man does, ordinary people will do; whatever standard he sets everyone will follow."

"The person who has made an indelible mark on my life is Richard Anderson. I've known and worked with Richard for more than twenty years. He is a leader with incredible wisdom and able to grasp any topic, to the point of very quickly becoming an expert. He is able to engage at any level to fully understand issues, technologies, methods of analyses, etc.

Richard taught me that you can never stop learning and can control your learning. You have the experts around you, and as a leader you should always feel comfortable leaning on the experience and knowledge of others.

Richard also taught me the power of humility and loyalty. Without question, as the CEO of Delta, he was one of the most influential and successful airline leaders over the past several decades. Twenty years ago Richard made a personal commitment to support my career growth. He never wavered from that commitment. He is loyal, a man of his word, and keeps his deals.

His lasting impact on me is that no matter how much is demanded of your time, you never, ever compromise your values. In fact, great and lasting success comes only when you are able to effectively align those values with the way you live your life and carry out your career."

William L. Lentsch
Senior Vice President, Delta Air Lines

Now, of course, choosing Right Action every day is far from easy, for it means trusting the outcome. In a pressure-packed, performance-oriented world, there are many forces that seek to influence our choices. The outcomes of Right Action may not appear at first glance to be in our best interests. Right Action, therefore, is often courageous action because it might mean taking an unpopular stand for what is honest and just.

Right Action can also serve as 'corrective' action as when we catch ourselves behaving inconsistently with our values but then change course to protect our integrity. During a corrective phase, it is instructive to consider the long-term effects of wrong action; our news is full of celebrated athletes, politicians, and businesspeople whose reputations have been destroyed by misguided ambition and the use of unscrupulous actions to achieve their ends.

Correspondingly, through consistent Right Action, character is developed, and impeccable reputations are built. Warren Buffett, one of the richest people in the world, and someone who exemplifies Right Action, stated, "If you get to my age in life, and nobody thinks well of you, I don't care how big your bank account is, your life is a disaster."

So, as we contemplate the three steps we have just discussed in this chapter—taking charge of your thoughts, words, and actions—it is important to understand that perfection has never been our goal. The goal has always been to encourage growth and progress. With that as your focus, the willingness to consistently practice these three steps will leave you amazed at your growing confidence. You will be amazed by your sense of tranquility, you will be amazed at how your 'buttons' are not so easily pushed, and you will become aware that life is an amazing gift that you get to open every day.

"Do stuff, be clenched, curious. Not waiting for inspiration's shove or society's kiss on your forehead. Pay attention. It's all about paying attention. Attention is vitality. It connects you with others. It makes you eager. Stay eager."

—Susan Sontag

Stepping into the Mystery

7

Life is difficult, life is amazing. Life is challenging, life is astonishing. Life is painful, life is joyous.

Life can be amazing, yet life can be difficult. Life is abundant with opportunity, yet has many challenges. Life can be full of joy, yet is often painful. At any point in our lives, one of these statements could accurately describe what we are experiencing. As I have endeavored to make sense of the complexity of my own life, I have concluded that life has a mystery to it that I for one will never fully understand.

This conclusion has led me to believe that to live fully and expansively requires some sort of faith, the purpose of which is to provide us with the courage and resilience to push on. There are many who share this belief, and of course, plenty who do not. The essence of what I believe

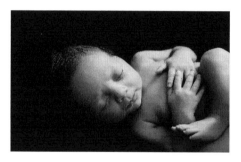

is captured in this statement by the philosopher and theologian, Pierre Teilhard de Chardin: "We are not human beings having a spiritual experience. We are spiritual beings having a human experience."

Those words resonate with me. What it means to be a spiritual being, however, extends far beyond the ambitions of this book. It is a broad and dynamic conversation that can range from a belief in a god, a higher power, a creative force, the Tao, and many other definitions. Some people do not believe in any sort of god but can embrace a belief in the endurance and power of the human spirit.

I do believe in God, which I have come to perceive as an imaginative, creative, life-giving spirit existing and permeating through all of nature—of which human beings are a part. I am not threatened, however, by anyone who argues that there is not a god. Many times, I have personally questioned and doubted the existence of a god.

I am also an advocate for science and its discipline of requiring fact-based evidence, and it is such evidence that has significantly influenced my beliefs. That being said, the words from Shakespeare's *Hamlet* echo in my ears: "There are more things in heaven and earth, Horatio, than are dreamt of in your philosophy."

...love and compassion triumph...

It is the events and experiences of life that have left me with the conviction that some transcendent 'presence' exists. When I witness love and compassion triumph over hate and revenge, when I watch the astrophysicist and cosmologist Neil de Grasse Tyson describe the awesome grandeur of an ever-expanding universe, when my whole being responds with a sense of peace and serenity as I listen to Pachelbel's *Canon in D*, my reactions come from a place within me that I feel is beyond the blood, tissue, and wiring of my brain and body.

These thoughts necessitate clarifying the objective of this chapter. It is by no means an attempt to convert anyone to what I have come to believe. It is about creating greater awareness, stimulating new insights, and opening new vistas that have consistently been the goals of our work together. With this in mind, I believe that achieving these goals necessitates an exploration into the mystery of life.

To not have this conversation and share my own spiritual journey would, I feel, not only leave our time together incomplete, it would leave out the key context in which I hold my life. My spirituality frames my worldview, my purpose, and approach to each day. Ultimately, it is the answer to how I perceive the reason for my existence and the mark I wish to leave on the world.

There is also a selfish motive. Every one of us has an inner life—some more private or secret than others. I hope that one day my grandchildren will read this book and discover a window into the inner life of their grandfather. Granted, it may be many years before this happens, but as we get

older we become more interested in knowing about what influenced our ancestors—the sources of both our beliefs, genes, and family cultures.

As I have previously revealed, I was born in London, England, and that is where my awareness of the spiritual aspect of life began. By the time I was seven I had become an altar boy at All Hallows Catholic Church in Devons Road, Bow. Those were great days—incense flying around everywhere, bells ringing ceremoniously, the Mass in Latin... a language I did not understand, and the wine, yes... real wine.

As an immigrant to Australia with my parents at the age of nine, I soon learned that, despite Australia being founded as a British penal colony, there was a distinct Aussie version of English. In fact, if you see some Australian movies today, many have sub-titles. "G'day" is a well-known greeting, but how about "Ooroo" which means goodbye, or "Fair dinkum" which means I'm telling you the truth.

Children have a strong need to fit in with new friends and environments. I soon mastered the language and, once again, entered the ranks of the altar boys. The Mass was still in Latin, and I quickly learned even Aussie kids didn't understand what was going on.

At thirteen I took an almighty leap. The Christian Brothers at my all-boys high school were thrilled when I told them I felt I had a vocation to the priesthood. Always looking for recruits, they soon whisked me away to a seminary. In those days, entering a seminary so young was not unusual. It was done with the full approval of parents, although my mother laughingly told me later that she never could get her head around how being a priest reconciled with my other desire of being a movie star!

At that time, seminarians were completely cut off from the outside world. Only weekly hikes into the surrounding hills and valleys provided a reprieve from the monastic life. Occasionally we would come across a group of girls from a local boarding school also out hiking, and it was from those chance encounters that I got the first inkling that being a priest may not be for me.

The ultimate evidence, however, was that even at that young age ambition was my middle name. I slowly came to the realization that I really did not want to be a priest. I actually wanted to be the pope, and as there had been few non-Italian popes elected at that time the chances of an Aussie being chosen were slim. After a year I was back in the secular world.

In the transition to becoming an adult I found myself questioning many of the traditional beliefs of my childhood. Fortunately, I had parents who did not try to restrict my thinking. They encouraged personal growth, were curious and inquisitive themselves, and were open to considering multiple points of view. This allowed me to go on a wonderful adventure to discover what resonated with my own soul.

On my journey I was exposed to and explored the teachings of the world's great religions. My most important discovery was that whilst there were clear differences there were many commonalities. Whether it was Jesus, Buddha, Muhammad, Lao Tzu, or Confucius, each was providing direction, principles, inspiration, and wisdom for how to be both more effective in managing our lives and how to live a more meaningful life. In other words, and of great significance to me, these lessons were highly oriented to the here and now, to the life we are currently living.

...each was providing inspiration and wisdom.

What was remarkably absent from what was being taught was the imposition of shame, guilt, and punishment for our 'sins.' These negative elements appear to have been unfolded and gained greater emphasis as religious institutions emerged. The negative focus often dominated, superseding the beauty and intent of the original teachings.

Those teachings were clearly about love, acceptance, peace, humility, and possibility. Of great importance to me, as I discussed in Chapter 1, was the role of forgiveness. These are the teachings that now influence my spirituality. Teachings lead to practices, and these practices create a world to which most people aspire.

So, in these times when religious fanaticism tends to dominate the headlines, and where other less militant, yet self-righteous groups, create divisions between people, communities, and countries, I align with and support those who work to educate and eliminate the ignorance and prejudice that is so prevalent.

An inspiring example of this effort was featured in an issue of *Science of Mind* magazine. Julie Mierau writes about The Interfaith Amigos, a pastor, a rabbi, and an imam. Together they are collaborating to create a rich dialog among different faith communities. The objective is to help us learn, despite our individual belief systems, how much, at the deepest level, "We are," as Maya Angelou wrote, "more alike, my friends, than we are unalike."

Each of the Amigos brings his own perspective to the conversation. Rabbi Ted Falco states, "People often seek the security of certainty... The ego strives to avoid vulnerability by attaching itself to absolutes. But that is a dangerous and costly strategy." Imam Jamal Rahman offers, "There are issues in every religion that can be used to promote polarization. To overcome that polarization, we have to do the spiritual work. We must overcome our egos and open our hearts." Pastor Don Mackenzie says, "For whatever reason, some people are more in touch with the truth that we are connected. They see that the distance between us is an illusion."

The approach of the Interfaith Amigos aligns with my spiritual philosophy. It is inclusive. Every human being comes from the same source. DNA research shows that, at a most fundamental level, we can all, in fact, be defined as 'cousins.' I have interacted and worked with people who represent nearly every race and region of the world, and to me the fact that our intrinsic, human needs and motivations are fundamentally the same is unquestionable.

Now, do I condone the outrageous behavior of some of these 'cousins'? Of course not. I am appalled and heartbroken by the cruelty we witness in the world. Do I believe that people should be held accountable and experience consequences for their actions? Absolutely! But what I do know is that when we shift our focus from these negative acts, we discover that those who are committed to creating a better world overwhelmingly outnumber those who would destroy it.

My personal beliefs have been formed, as with each of us, by what I have been exposed to and experienced. There are no protective walls around my beliefs, and I have no need to defend them. They are framed in such a way that questions can be asked, other points of view heard, and fresh conclusions arrived at. I realize that this openness would be uncomfortable for many, but rigidity in one's thinking is anathema to me. I love exploring unanswered questions, and the older I get the more questions there are.

"The person who made an indelible mark on my life is a fellow pastor at my church, Bob Brinkley. Bob is well into his eighties and is a life-long learner and spiritual seeker and has been since I met him nearly thirty years ago. He has continued to evolve into his most authentic self and encourages others to do the same. Bob's lasting legacy to me has been to keep reaching, to keep going deeper, and to keep being open to the beautiful possibilities of life and all its gifts."

—Reverend Sally Johnson – Hennepin Avenue United Methodist Church

You might wonder if I attend a church service regularly. The answer is yes. In fact, there is rarely a Sunday morning when I am not there. It is a community that reflects my values and beliefs and a place where everyone is truly welcome no matter your creed, your lifestyle, or history. It is an environment of love and healing. Doubts are accepted, the conversation is rich, and judgment is non-existent. As we leave we feel inspired and courageous. We are nourished and nurtured. The purpose is fulfilled.

It is not easy to travel your own spiritual path. There is safety in certainty and discomfort when long-held beliefs are challenged. It takes courage to ask questions even when your instincts tell you that something is amiss, that there are many contradictions, and perhaps there may be a more enriching and satisfying spiritual path you could follow.

As we leave... we are nourished and nurtured.

The television program *God in America* was particularly insightful in exploring different paths. One story described the efforts of Spanish missionaries to convert the Pueblo Indians of New Mexico from their 'pagan' ways. A key problem was that the missionaries lived in a world of absolutes. Their dogma left no room for dialog.

This eventually created an untenable situation. The Pueblos had been practicing a very relevant and practical spirituality for a thousand years, and now they were being told it was wrong. Many Pueblos resisted the new teachings and were subsequently treated harshly. The Pueblos eventually rebelled by the thousands, and the missionaries were forced to flee.

What is this practical spirituality of the Pueblos? During the *God in America* program, a contemporary Pueblo Indian stated it clearly: "Our whole world is our religion. Our way of life is our religion. The way we act toward one another is our religion. From the moment we wake up until we go to bed and when we are sleeping, that is our religion." In other words, the Pueblos spiritual life framed their whole life. There was no compartmentalization. To use a modern vernacular, they lived their religion 24/7.

The Aboriginal people of Australia have a unique spirituality that can be traced back more than thirty thousand years. There is no book such as the Bible or Talmud or Koran that documents their beliefs. How the world came to be and what is sacred to them has been handed down orally from generation to generation and is known as *The Dreamtime*.

When asked to describe *The Dreamtime*, an Aboriginal elder said, "It's hard to explain—dreaming is a very big thing!" It is very "big" because *The Dreamtime* is the story of how the universe and everything in it was created.

It includes a clear description of the natural laws that govern the universe and human relationships.

According to Aboriginal belief, when walking on the land one must tread lightly for we walk on the Mother. Do no harm. There is no need for unnecessary or loud noises. That is an interesting notion in our modern world where noise is so intrusive and pervasive.

Of even greater relevance is that *The Dreamtime* teaches that there is a reason for creation and a purpose to life. Australian Aborigines, similar to Native Americans, believe everything is connected. They believe your personal dreams provide insight into your relationship with the universe. I don't unconditionally accept these beliefs, but I find it intriguing that current dream research suggests that one purpose of our dreams is to help process our emotions. The failure to process emotions leads to anxiety and worry.

Exploring the spirituality of ancient cultures reveals a treasure trove of wisdom, a wisdom that demonstrates that the mystery of life has occupied the thoughts of humans for thousands of years. This wisdom encourages us to break from the confines of so many of our ingrained beliefs and to think expansively.

...the spirituality of ancient cultures reveals a treasure...

This wisdom also leads to what matters, and, in terms of human existence, what truly matters seems to have remained remarkably consistent. A powerful example is the way Australian Aboriginal children are taught. Contained within *The Dreamtime* there is an ethics system known as the Wudu teachings.

According to Munya Andrews, an Aboriginal writer and historian, to whose work I am indebted for much of what I am sharing with you, Wudu is taught around the campfire at dawn and dusk when the slanted rays of Mother Sun are believed to be powerful and most influential.

Either parents or grandparents first warm their hands by the fire and then sequentially touch different parts of the child's body. Touching the child's hands represents the need for honesty. They say, "Don't steal what is not yours."

Touching the forehead is the warning to never believe that you are more important than others. They say, "Don't let your forehead swell." When the eyes are touched they are implored to not be busybodies, to only see and mind their own business.

When the mouth is touched they are told to avoid gossip or saying bad things about other people. Above all, Wudu teaches the value of sharing and caring for one another throughout life and the importance of contributing to the community.

It is fascinating and worthy of deep reflection that in this world of instant communication through Twitter, Instagram, Facebook, and other Internet tools, many of the most meaningful answers to a life that matters are to be found in the spiritual beliefs of people and their cultures that have existed since the history of human beings was first recorded.

"Mystery creates wonder," said the famous astronaut, Neil Armstrong, "and wonder is the basis of man's desire to understand."

Take time now to reflect upon and describe your own spirituality. This exercise can take many directions. It could reflect your religion or aspects of the faith you practice. It could be your world view. It could be your values and how you see the reason or purpose for your existence, or it could be a combination of the above elements. Through examining what we believe, we can explore how our beliefs serve us in living courageous and imaginative lives.

My spirituality:

As you consider what you have just written, remember that this book is about how you will leave a positive mark on the world. That requires being willing to explore beliefs and assumptions, to be open, to be curious, to listen, to question, and to be willing, as fans of *Star Trek* would understand, "To boldly go where no man has gone before."

So how might you assess your spiritual path? Consider these questions:

Does the path you're following inspire you with possibilities?

Does it empower you to be courageous?

Does it provide comfort in troubling times?

Is it aligned with what your life's experiences have taught you?

If you can answer yes to each of these questions, I am pleased for what that means for you. If you cannot, I encourage you to continue to explore until you discover that inner 'source' to which you can connect when you need the strength to push on or the inspiration to become all you desire to be.

...the mystery that permeates my own experience.

My personal conviction of the existence of a God has, however, ultimately not come from a book, a service, or a sermon. It has come from what has occurred in my life that is beyond human understanding—the mystery that permeates my own experiences.

Here is one.

What do we do when we lose a beloved wife and partner, a person who brought rich companionship for many years, and with whom many tears and uncountable laughs have been shared?

What occurs to me now—more than a decade after my wife, Jo, passed away—is that to succeed in getting up every day and moving forward in life necessitates embracing the unfathomable, the unanswerable, and the inexplicable.

A week after Jo's funeral in Minneapolis I flew to Australia to be with my father and brothers. I was exhausted from several months of intense caregiving and the emotions associated with watching a loved one slowly fade away. Leaving the harsh Minnesota winter, I was primed to begin healing in the warm sunshine of the city where I had grown up and got married.

One morning I was walking the beaches on which Jo and I had spent so much of our young lives, and as the grief counselors would advise, I was speaking to her as if she were alive. I took it one step further, however, and decided to ask questions. Now did I expect answers? Not really, but they came back as if we were in a regular, albeit ethereal conversation.

First question: "You know I thought I would be a mess, but although I've shed many tears I'm not feeling too bad right now. How do you account for that?" Immediately, came this response: "David, I am very happy, and I want you to be happy." I was astonished, and my rational side was fighting what I had just heard. *Surely my mind is playing games,* I thought.

Let me check this out. I tried a second question, but this time I brought in the sense of humor we had both shared. "I must admit I'm a little envious of you. There you are probably having a cup of tea in the morning with your mum and dad and a martini with my mother in the afternoon. Why am I still here?"

She answered, "David, because you still have work to do!"

Now, I am fully aware of how this internal conversation can be justified. Was Jo actually communicating with me? When one's emotions are raw I assure you that does not matter. What I clearly know is that this encounter, as mysterious as it was, brought me incredible comfort, and to a grieving person, that does matter.

I still have work to do.

As time has passed, the message has not been forgotten. I still have work to do. My mission on earth is not finished. There is more to learn, more to experience, and more to accomplish, and even though I have moved beyond the grief associated with my loss, those words heard on a beach in a time of despair continue to be the most meaningful answer to why I am still alive.

"The time has come to redefine ourselves.

We are not our memories,

Important though they are.

We are not our bodies,

Familiar though they are.

There is something else here,

Mysterious and elusive.

What is it?"

—William Martin – The Sage's Tao Te Ching

One Precious Life

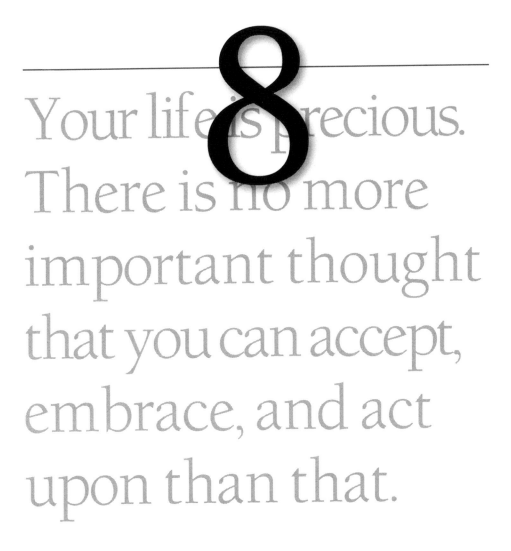

Your life is precious.
There is no more
important thought
that you can accept,
embrace, and act
upon than that.

The revered poet, Mary Oliver, completes her poem, *The Summer Day*, with these words: "Tell me, what is it you plan to do with your one wild and precious life?"

This question holds as much power and meaning for me as ever. If I still have work to do what will that look like? How will I treasure the days and years ahead? Where will I focus my energy? How will I contribute? What will I create? To whom will I look for inspiration? Who will be my role models?

If you are young and wondering if you still need role models at seventy, the answer is—absolutely! I assure you that Tony Bennett, at age eighty-eight, recording an album with Lady Gaga is very motivating to me. The creative force within us expires only when we expire.

The creative force within us expires only when we expire.

The relevance of Mary Oliver's question is particularly striking when I observe my grandchildren. As I complete this work, two are in college, two are in kindergarten, and one is in pre-school. All I see is pure potential. My prayer is that they will be inspired to fully express their gifts and talents and make their own enduring mark on the world.

This is also my wish for you, no matter your stage in life. "Life is either a daring adventure, or nothing at all," said Helen Keller. Strong words from a woman who was the first deaf-blind person to earn a bachelor of arts degree, but that is the choice we face every day. Age is not a barrier; it is only an excuse.

My brother, Steve, whilst on a European cruise got into a conversation with a woman in her eighties. He discovered that she was perpetually on the move exploring as many countries as possible. Asked why she traveled so much, she responded, "I want to cover as much of the earth as I can, before the earth covers me."

One precious life. Do we realize the magnitude of this gift? Have we been awakened to how exhilarating life can be? Most important of all, can we summon the courage to take charge of our lives, put away the excuses, and experience that exhilaration? As hard as this may be to accept, if our lives are mundane, we have only ourselves to blame.

If our lives are mundane, we have only ourselves to blame.

Leaving our mark on the world requires much more than a somewhat thoughtless daily routine that can only be described as existence. It demands that we raise our consciousness to a whole new level, to think and act in ways that enable us to soar above mediocrity and all that would bind us to a limited life. "Follow your bliss," said Joseph Campbell, "and the universe will open doors for you where there were only walls."

It was his grandmother, a village healer, who inspired Alfred Quinones-Hinojosa to make the most of his own wild and precious life. Born into a poor family in Mexico, he arrived in the United States at the age of nineteen. Speaking no English, Alfred took a job pulling weeds in the tomato and cotton fields of California's San Joaquin Valley.

From attending literacy classes at a community college he evolved into a teacher of fellow immigrants. A mentor who

ran a Hispanic Center of Excellence saw his potential and how well he connected with people and encouraged Alfred to enter the world of medicine. His grades enabled him to attend Harvard Medical School where he graduated *cum laude*.

Today, Dr. Quinones-Hinojosa is the Chair of Neurologic Surgery for the Mayo Institute's medical center in Jacksonville, Florida, and a movie is being made about his life story. As a young nineteen-year-old, however, this possibility was beyond his wildest dreams. For that reason, he never fails to give credit to those who supported him throughout his remarkable life's journey.

In a talk at the University of Guadalajara, he said, "I left a peasant. I came back a professor. As you go up in life, you should always look back and help the people behind you."

Alfred Quinones-Hinojosa—*One precious life.*

Ravishanka Gundlapalli, a successful entrepreneur who was born in India, tells the story of a young man who showed him the difference between sight and vision. After he had delivered a keynote address at the Indian School of Business in Hyderabad, India, a student approached him and shared his dream of becoming an engineer, but there was a major challenge. The student was visually impaired, and universities in India would not accept an engineering student with this disability.

Not to be thwarted in his quest, the young man told Ravi that he had set his 'sights' on MIT, one of the most prestigious universities in the world, located in Cambridge, Massachusetts.

It was a bold, audacious goal.

It was a bold, audacious goal which so impressed Ravi that he decided to become a mentor to the student.

Building on an excellent academic record, having an incredible determination, and guided by Ravi's advice and counsel, the young student was eventually interviewed at MIT and accepted with a full scholarship. Ravi fully acknowledges his mentee for his clarity of vision and persistence, but adds the following: "I have come to realize a beautiful aspect about mentoring—the knowledge we possess may seem obvious to us but can be a game changer and eye-opener for someone else when delivered with the right intent at the right time."

The ripple effect of this relationship is profound. The student has launched a social venture that provides students with disabilities the support they need to achieve their goals. Ravi, building on the evidence of the undeniable need for and benefits of mentorship, has created MentorCloud, a company committed to ensuring that those who need a knowledgeable and caring mentor will find them.

Ravishanka Gundlapalli—*One precious life.*

Sarah Longacre was far from being an A student. Just graduating from college, in fact, was a major achievement. Hired by Nike, she spent the first few years of her career working in marketing at Nike's headquarters in Portland, Oregon. Her true passions, however, lay elsewhere. A yoga practitioner, she had also been trained as a Doula, a woman who assists other women during childbirth and who often provides support to the family after the baby is born.

Sarah began to sense that these two disciplines had powerful synergies. She knew that the presence of a Doula brought a comforting reassurance to the vulnerability felt especially by a new mother. The exercise and meditative aspects of yoga strengthened the mother both physically

and emotionally and enabled her to be more prepared for childbirth. Her instincts proved right.

Returning to her home in Minnesota to be closer to family, Sarah began to envision a business built on meeting these synchronous needs. After testing her theory with several groups, she was left with no doubt that the opportunity was substantial. Soon Blooma, a pre- and post-natal yoga studio that provides education and wellness services, was born. Young mothers-to-be flocked to participate.

Blooma studios are now being established throughout the United States and other countries, and Sarah is creating a unique clothing line for the Blooma customer and greater population.

Whilst Sarah Longacre is unquestionably a success story, she has not escaped personal tragedy. Pregnant with her second child, the baby was born prematurely and did not survive. Her grief was deep, but she has transformed this experience into an even greater sense of purpose and commitment to the community Blooma serves. One client wrote: "You challenged me, you comforted me, you reminded me that we are all here with stories and heartbreaks. We are all sad and scared as well as hopeful and joyful."

Sarah Longacre—*One precious life.*

Bill Cunningham had no grand designs to change the world or be someone of 'importance.' He just wanted to live his life on his own terms. Ironically, he was continually sought after by the rich and powerful. Described by Arthur Ochs Sulzberger Jr., the chairman and publisher of the *New York Times*, as being, "One of the kindest, most gentle people I have met," Cunningham worked for the *Times* as a fashion photographer for close to forty years.

Although revered by his colleagues, Cunningham preferred as much anonymity as he could get. His subjects were not models on a catwalk; they were people he saw on the street or at events where he could unobtrusively capture a person's individual style and spirit. He once said, "At parties, it's important to be almost invisible, to catch people when they're oblivious to the camera, to get the intensity of their speech, the gestures of their hands." His focus was always his subjects. He had no need for personal recognition.

Bill Cunningham became a superstar in New York by default. He resisted most every attempt to celebrate him and participated reluctantly in a documentary about his life and work. Regarded as a highly ethical journalist, those who had the privilege to meet or be photographed by Bill Cunningham also were impacted by his unique combination of humility, commitment, and passion.

The mark he left was summed up by a friend: "We will all miss his talent, his eye, and his kindness. How we look at style won't be the same without the inimitable Bill Cunningham."

Bill Cunningham—*One precious life.*

144

In the preface of this book are these words: "Leaving your mark is not a goal to be set—it is a result. It is the outcome of realizing the enormous potential that exists within you, the belief that there is a special purpose for your existence, the awareness that you share responsibility for what happens in our world, and the commitment to fully use your gifts and talents to live a rich and rewarding life."

> # Leaving your mark is not a goal to be set.

"When people die," said Oliver Sacks, "they cannot be replaced. They leave holes that cannot be filled, for it is the fate—the genetic and neural fate—of every human being to be a unique individual, to find his own path, to live his own life..." That has been the purpose of our work together—to value and appreciate your uniqueness to discover your own path and to create a *One Precious Life* that fully expresses who you are.

That need to express who we are doesn't change no matter our age. There is no planet called *Made It*. Just as when we gaze up into the evening sky and see an ever-expanding universe, so does age and life present the opportunities for even more exciting discoveries. I may have to give in to the realities of an older body, but never will I give up on developing an even greater capacity for love and learning.

This leads to the revealing of a special gift I have been blessed with these past several years. Her name is Cheryl, and as you read these words, she will have become my wife. Would I have thought this possible after the loss of Jo? It was not in my wildest dreams, but love is truly infinite. The words of Loretta Young describe our union perfectly: "Love isn't something you find. Love is something that finds you."

You and I are most likely at very different stages in our lives and careers. With that in mind, I have endeavored to ensure that what has been written about and the exercises you have been asked to complete are relevant no matter at what stage you might be.

Perhaps, however, life has already taught you that motivations, values, and priorities evolve and change from decade to decade. In the book to which I have referred several times, *The Sage's Tao Te Ching*, the Chinese philosopher, Confucius, is quoted as saying, "At fifteen, I was committed to learning. At thirty, I took my rightful position. At forty, I was no longer totally perplexed. At fifty, I began to understand the unfolding of my true nature. At sixty, I was in harmony with contradictions and ambivalence. At seventy, at long last, I could follow my heart's desire without going astray."

Motivations, values and priorities evolve...

But even at seventy life is still about choices. This morning, as I write these words, I have chosen to communicate with you. It is a wonderful moment. Wonderful memories come from wonderful moments. There are only a few more paragraphs to go, and my vision for writing a new book will be achieved. My experience assures me that this two-year journey will translate into a marvelous sense of accomplishment.

Then what? When I wake up in the morning to discover that I am still alive, will I practice what I preached to you throughout these pages? My commitment is that we will always be fellow travelers in embracing this one precious life. Here is why.

"David, I believe we can safely say you're cured!" Those words uttered by my surgeon at the Mayo Clinic were both unexpected and stunning. It had been five years since the removal of the malignant tumor and the discovery of my cancer. Statistically, the five-year mark is significant if one is to survive cancer.

"We can safely say you're cured!"

In the cancer world, however, "cure" is a monumental word. It is much bigger than "remission" and towers above "cancer free." I looked at this man whom I believed had saved my life and asked, "Cured?"

"Yes, cured," he repeated.

A tsunami of emotion swept over me. Immense gratitude tumbled around with the implications of this amazing news.

Every six months for five years I had been visiting my surgeon and oncologist and had been subjected to PET scans and extensive examinations of my ears, nose, and throat. Each time the visit would be concluded with the words, "You're doing good." I would let out a sigh of relief and head back into the fray of life. At the back of my mind, however, was always the thought—*next time something may be found.*

I am now convinced that this concern constrained me. Although it may not have been observable to others, my willingness to take risks had certainly been contained, and I found myself playing safe, which was not my normal *modus operandi.* Now, however, what would be my excuse or rationale for holding back?

This was the thought that preoccupied me as I drove home from the Mayo. When so many do not survive cancer, why me? A philosophical answer to that question appears to be true for all of us: if we're alive, our mission on earth isn't finished. But as one approaching seventy, how big a vision was reasonable for me?

It was to be just a few minutes before I found out. I described in Chapter 3 the phenomenon of synchronicity—a meaningful coincidence. It is an unexpected and totally surprising connection to a life event one is confronting or experiencing. Synchronicity is often a spark or source of encouragement, inspiration, and insight when most needed.

If we're alive, our mission on earth isn't finished.

Let me describe the scene. As I continued the drive home, and to ensure I kept to the speed limit, my car was on cruise control. My thoughts, however, remained obsessed with the question of *what now*?

At one point, in the distance, I saw an image hovering directly above the highway. As I drew closer, there, no more than forty feet above the car, was a magnificent eagle. For the few seconds this creature was in my vision, time seemed to stop. I could see every facet so clearly—the proud head and glorious wings. I have never been so close to this symbol with which my work has so long been associated.

"Look at me, David," the eagle seemed to imply. "We have meant so much to each other. Our partnership has influenced the lives of thousands of people. Let us use this gift of new life and recommit ourselves to the purpose for which we were created. Let us create a bold new vision of what we can contribute to this world."

Yes, I will always be on this journey with you. For now, however, I leave you with these thoughts.

Over the years I have learned to accept my limitations, my weaknesses, and my laughable idiosyncrasies. I have also been willing to acknowledge and validate my strengths. The world, I have discovered, is full of ambiguity, contradictions, and millions of people whose philosophy does not connect to mine. There is one thing, however, about which I'm certain—each of our lives *is* precious.

Of all the questions you have answered throughout this book, there is only one that ultimately matters—what *will* you do with your one wild and precious life?

There is no more important thought you can embrace than that your life is precious. You have great value. The world needs you. Through your contribution, through your determination

What will you do with your one wild and precious life?

to live your life fully, through your learning and growing, your indelible mark is left, and we are all the beneficiaries.

List of References

Resources

Books

Even Eagles Need a Push—David McNally

The Eagle's Secret—David McNally

Be Your Own Brand—David McNally and Karl Speak

The Push—David McNally

My Sacred Journey Through Cancer—David McNally

Bhagavad Gita—Steven Mitchell translation

Brands and Branding—The Economist

Creating—Robert Fritz

Finding Each Other in Judaism—Harold M. Schulweis

Forgiveness—Sidney B. Simon and Suzanne Simon

Good to Great—Jim Collins

Lovemarks—Kevin Roberts

Married to the Brand—William J McEwen

The Pause—Kevin Cashman

The Phenomenon of Man—Pierre Teilhard de Chardin

The Road Less Traveled—M. Scott Peck

The Sage's Tao Te Ching—William Martin

The Talent Code—Daniel Coyle

The Ultimate Question—Fred Reichheld

Films

The Power of Purpose—Documentary about Terry Fox

If I Were Brave—Documentary of people successfully transcending adversity

Audio Books

Even Eagles Need a Push—David McNally

The Eagle's Secret—David McNally

Be Your Own Brand—David McNally and Karl Speak

David McNally

International Business Speaker—Author—Thought Leader

 For over forty years, David McNally has inspired millions of people from the stage, on film, and in his best-selling books. His following has garnered him the honor of election to the Speakers' Hall of Fame and recognition by a leading speakers' bureau as one of the world's Top 50 business speakers.

David is the author of the best-selling books, *Even Eagles Need a Push: Learning to Soar in a Changing World* and *The Eagle's Secret: Success Strategies for Thriving at Work and in Life.* His book *Be Your Own Brand* is used by many business schools throughout the world in their graduate degree programs. And now *Mark Of An Eagle: How Your Life Changes the World,* David's new book, brings fresh, inspiring insights and wisdom for creating a successful and meaningful life.

An award-winning producer, David has produced two highly praised, inspirational films, *The Power of Purpose* and *If I Were Brave.*

David's books have been translated into twelve languages and developed into corporate training programs released in over twenty countries. Abbott, Ameriprise, Apple Autos, Conway, Delta Air Lines, Gartner, Merrill Lynch, Pulte Homes, and Thrivent Financial are among the many distinguished organizations that have recognized David's work.

As founder and CEO of TransForm Corporation, David and his staff align leaders, teams, and individuals throughout organizations to build iconic brands.

For information on David McNally or
TransForm Corporation contact:

info@transformcorp.com | www.transformcorp.com | (952) 835-0300